TIES THAT BIND

**Familial Homophobia and
Its Consequences**

TIES THAT BIND

Familial Homophobia and Its Consequences

Sarah Schulman

THE NEW PRESS

NEW YORK
LONDON

Requests for permission to reproduce selections from this book should be
mailed to: Permissions Department, The New Press, 38 Greene Street,
New York, NY 10013.

Published in the United States by The New Press, New York, 2009
Distributed by Perseus Distribution

CIP data available
ISBN 978-1-59558-480-9 (hc)

The New Press was established in 1990 as a not-for-profit alternative to the large,
commercial publishing houses currently dominating the book publishing industry.
The New Press operates in the public interest rather than for private gain, and is
committed to publishing, in innovative ways, works of educational, cultural, and
community value that are often deemed insufficiently profitable.

www.thenewpress.com

Composition by dix!

Printed in the United States of America

10   9   8   7   6   5   4   3   2   1

Dedicated to those who keep their promises.

"We must understand and confront the unprecedented."

—Larry Kramer

CONTENTS

ACKNOWLEDGMENTS

Special thanks to the Corporation of Yaddo, the MacDowell Colony and Phil Wilkie. Thanks to the many readers. Deep appreciation to Alex Juhasz, my cousins Marcia Cohen-Zakai and Alon Zakai, Alix Dobkin, Dudley Saunders and Claudia Rankine.

TIES THAT BIND

Familial Homophobia and Its Consequences

INTRODUCTION

Familial Homophobia:
An Experience in Search of Recognition

Despite the emphasis on gay marriage and parenthood that has overwhelmed our current discourse, how gays and lesbians are treated IN families is far more influential on the quality of individual lives and the larger social order than how we are treated AS families. Yet, as is often the case, central and uncomfortable truths take a backseat to more facile and familiar conversations. In this book, I try to articulate how and why systems of familial homophobia operate, and, more importantly, how they can be changed.

There are two experiences that most homosexuals share. One is "coming out," a process of self-interrogation in opposition to social expectation that has no parallel in heterosexual life. The second common experience is that we have each, at some time in our lives, been treated shoddily by our families simply, but specifically, because of our homosexuality. This experience is, in turn, mirrored by the legal system and the dominant social structures within which gay people must live, as well as in the arts and entertainment industries, which select and control our representations. As a consequence, familial exclusion and diminishment is often extended by the behavior of gay people toward each other. It is a house of mirrors of enforcement.

Imagine if a family responded to the coming out of one of its members like this:

They discuss as a family their special responsibility to protect their daughter/sister/mother/niece/aunt/cousin from pressures and cruelties that they themselves will never face. They promise not to exploit or enjoy privileges that she is denied, and to commit their family's resources to accessing those privileges for her and other gay people. They extend this commitment to others in her community who don't have conscious, moral families. They treat those people like full human beings and support their gay family member in doing the same thing. In their larger family, friendships, workplaces, in their consumption or production of culture, in how they vote, and what laws they both support and access. They intervene when gay people are being scapegoated by directly addressing the perpetrators.

This is not an impossible scenario. Yet, today, families are more likely to "tolerate" homosexuals, that is, to keep them in a position of lesser value than to learn from them and be elevated by their knowledge. It is far more common to see a politician with an openly gay child actively opposing gay rights than to see him publicly praising that child for having the self-awareness and integrity to come out.

Because of the twisted nature of dominant behavior, gay people are being punished within the family structure even though we have not done anything wrong. This punishment has dramatic consequences on both our social experiences, and our most trusting, loving sexual relationships.

The specifics and dimensions of familial homophobia are broad and vast. They can range from short-sighted slights to varying degrees of exclusion to brutal attacks that distort the gay person's life to direct and indirect cruelties that literally end that person's existence. The impact of this will vary, of course, based on what other kinds of support systems the victim has been able to accrue, how committed the family is to enforcing the homophobia, and what kind of interventions are performed by third parties. If the family's prejudices are flexible, if the victim has consistent and reliable active support from others, and if other individuals in the family or community actively intervene to denounce, and therefore mitigate the impact of the cruelty, familial homophobia can be an unnecessary but overcomeable obstacle.

Without compassionate intervention, however, familial homophobia can become an overwhelmingly wrenching determinate on the gay person's life. Worse, it can be the model for the ways that gay people treat each other. History shows that recipients of undeserved cruelty—scapegoats— are dependent on the intervention of third parties to support their own acts of resistance. The weak need help. This often starts with a few individuals putting themselves between perpetrators and victims, and results ultimately in new kinds of social standards and sometimes legislation.

Strangely, the issues of this book are both obvious and denied. After all, it is being written in a moment when most people will tell you that "things are getting better" without being able to define, beyond banal cliché, what that actually means. The AIDS crisis forced America to start the process of acknowledging that gay people exist. Thus, even though there are many institutions today that still pretend that we do not exist, there are other institutions that acknowledge, in some form, that we do exist. This is a significant change, but not progress. In many states, cities, and counties, gay people can be fired from their jobs, kicked out of their homes, refused service in restaurants or hotels, denied membership in organizations and communities, and experience other victimizing humiliations. In five states (as of May 2009), gay and lesbian couples can be legally married. It's a bizarre set of daily contradictions that gay, lesbian, bisexual, and transgender people must balance and internalize. Some television shows have central characters who are homosexual; other television shows convey entire worlds in which homosexuality is never acknowledged. You never know what you're going to find around each corner.

However, the acknowledgment, when it does occur, is often problematic. Does the fact that openly gay people are allowed to have apartments in some places mean that "things are getting better?" Or does the fact that so many other places still protect discriminators reflect a more extreme cruelty today than it did forty years ago when gay nondiscrimination laws were unheard of?

I feel that the same negative action has a more intense negative meaning today than it did in the past, when there were fewer options for change. To oppose gay rights sixty years ago, when there was no visible movement, was a very different action than opposing us today. Knowing gay people, seeing our wish for justice, and saying "No" is a lot meaner than refusing something vague and theoretical. Although we are often told that "attitudes are changing for the better," I think we can all accept that when so many people in our country do not have legal rights and are not culturally represented, that is itself a condition of oppression. And that it reflects attitudes.

This twist, calling a constant state of injustice "progress," gets played out in a number of distorting ways. Most Americans now know that homosexuals exist. Simply representing us is falsely coded as "progress." Having a gay character in a book, play, film, or television show falsely codes that work as progressive. Often it even results in the work winning an award from a gay organization. But, if the actual meaning and content of the specific representation is examined, many of these representations are retrograde. They often portray the gay person as pathological, lesser than, a side-kick in the Tonto role, or there to provide an emotional catharsis to make the straight protagonist or viewer a "better" person. What current cultural representations rarely present are complex human beings with authority and sexuality, who are affected by homophobia in addition to their other human experiences, human beings who are *protagonists*. That type of depth and primacy would force audiences to universalize gay people, which is part of the equality process. It would also force an acknowledgment of heterosexual cruelty as a constant and daily part of American life.

These oppressive conventions and structures are kept in place by some concrete strategies. One crucial strategy is the use of false accusations to maintain gay people's subordinate status. False accusations are inaccurate and misleading statements about gay and lesbian people and about homosexuality that force us to live with the burden of a stigma that we don't deserve, and to then pay the emotional and social price of having to prove innocence that should not have to be proven.

The most typically vulgar false accusation homosexuals

face is that homosexuality is somehow wrong, and/or inferior to heterosexuality. This is a typical "smoke screen" kind of argument, an argument so ridiculous, and in fact insane, with no basis for justification, that to have to refute it is itself dehumanizing. We know the pattern: perpetrator falsely accuses victim in order to create a "smoke screen" that obscures the perpetrator's own agency. I say it is a "smoke screen" because, in addition to placing an unwarranted burden of proof on the gay person, it also obscures the real issue at hand, namely the perpetrator's homophobia.

Another typically vulgar false accusation is the charge that gay people should be kept away from children. Sadly, gay people have wasted a lot of energy and self-esteem in trying to prove how child-friendly we are. Even to the point of feeling that we have to have children to be fully human, or to be treated as fully human by our family or government. Today, in an act of diminishment, gay people use having children as proof that we deserve rights, respect, and representation. This of course reveals that our lack of children is a sign that something is wrong with us, that we are dangerous and deserve to be outside of power. This false accusation is another smoke screen, obscuring the real issue: that depriving children of relationships with gay people is itself child abuse. Especially for those children who are themselves gay and trapped within a family that practices or exploits homophobia.

These of course, are the most obvious and bottom-of-the-barrel false accusations, but there are also many more so-phisticated false accusations that are just as damaging.

For example:

- Homosexuals are a special interest group while heterosexuals are objective and neutral.
- Homosexuals' feelings are not as important as heterosexuals' feelings. (Extend this to artwork and social ideas.)
- Homosexuals have to prove that they are deserving of privileges that heterosexuals take for granted.
- Homosexuals should universalize to heterosexuals in order to enjoy representation, but heterosexuals should not have to show any interest outside of their own experience.
- Acquisition of rights and social change for gay people is their responsibility alone.

And my favorite and the most devolved:

- Gay and lesbian people, despite having no rights and no representation, somehow only achieve what we do because we are given unfair advantages: "Even though you have published ten books, you only got the job because they needed a lesbian."

I cannot tell you how many times straight people assume that I have professional advantages because I am a lesbian, when in fact it is the opposite. I have profound professional disadvantages because I am out in my work, and they have profound advantages because they are straight. This is the twist of course: to position advantages as neutral and any accomplishment as a benevolent gift from tolerant superiors.

And even more sophisticated:

- When any gay person, no matter how supremely achieved and deserving, receives some acknowledgment, this means that gay people have achieved equality. Or as a white woman once said to me, "What do you mean black people have no rights? Jesse Jackson has more power than my husband!"

Ironically, if gay people were treated equitably, the perpetrator would have the burden of proof. If they were made to account for their false accusations, it would be a lot harder to pull them off. Unfortunately, the system is twisted so that the cruelty looks normative and regular, and the desire to address and overturn it looks strange.

As Bertolt Brecht said, "As crimes pile up, they become invisible."

Resistance gets falsely pegged as the inappropriate behavior because it results in discomfort for the perpetrator. Ironically, it is often not the fact that a gay person is being scapegoated that makes people angry but the assertion that the perpetrator should have to be accountable that infuriates them. It's not the awful truth that upsets people, but the telling of the truth that gets construed as the problem.

While false accusation is a strategy of homophobia, shunning is its tool of enforcement. Shunning is when people are cut out, excluded from participating in conversations, communities, social structures; are not allowed to have any say about how they are treated; and cannot speak or speak back. Shunning is a form of mental cruelty that is designed to pretend that the victim does not exist and has never existed. It is practiced by religious groups like the Amish and Jehovah's Witnesses, but it is also practiced by the arts and entertainment industries, the legal system, family structures, economic systems, and social conventions that pathologize and isolate gay people by not acknowledging or representing our experiences. And, by extension, by irresponsible individuals who don't want to be accountable for the undeserved pain they are inflicting on others who don't have the power to create consequences. In short, shunning is an active form of harassment.

Because gay people are ritually shunned in all aspects of social life, dehumanizing us through shunning appears normative and regular. Even by other homosexuals. It's imitative.

Shunning is the most common form of homophobia and the easiest to carry out. While shunning seems passive and can be practiced daily without effort, its effects are dramatically active. In fact, being on the receiving end of shunning is to be aggressively assaulted on a daily basis. This can range from not acknowledging a gay family member's experiences and achievements as equal to those of other family members, to excluding authentic lesbian characters from the American stage. It's an exclusion system that can be manifested by making a gay family member uncomfortable while welcoming a straight family member, deciding that only one lesbian teacher can be hired in a department at a time or that no novels with lesbian protagonists can be published by a particular publishing house, by a lover deciding she has no accountability to her partner because no one else cares if she does or not. It is a removal of living, breathing people from recognition and representation in daily life. It is a refusal to engage, recognize, negotiate, communicate. It is an exclusion from the conversation.

Shunning is multiplicative. For example, in one week I can be excluded from a family event, be ignored by a publisher who has never published a lesbian novel, be disrespected by a theater that has never produced a lesbian play, and be denied job and housing protection in many states of the union. And let me add, many of my weeks look like this. If any of these parties felt that I had social currency or power, or that someone would care about how I was treated, their behavior would be different because they would fear the consequences. But, because all of these arenas agree that I don't matter, they can replicate and extend each other's habit of shunning and make it look normal and uneventful.

When people are put on the receiving end of a cruelty that they do not deserve, that is injustice. An intervention that makes perpetrators justify what they are doing can usually end that behavior. An intervention shows perpetrators that someone cares about their victim, about how she is treated and what becomes of her. It is undeniable that people only scapegoat the powerless. Those with power would never be falsely blamed; there would be consequences. For this reason, third party intervention is the most effective way of ending shunning. To intervene is to realign power. The bully can easily find another victim whom no one cares about. Why bother hurting someone who either has enough currency to fight back or an ally to fight back for them?

What makes gay people so ideal as the scapegoat in a family is that they are there alone. Sometimes no one else inside the family is like them or identifies with them. They become a projection screen, the dumping ground for everyone else's inadequacies and resentments. In addition, no one else is watching. No one from the outside will intervene because of the perception that family matters are private and untouchable. The family structure and its untouchability predominates. Then, because gay people do not have the full support of their families, they in turn become an ideal social scapegoat. For, in society, just as in the family, no one will intervene. Society will not intervene in the family, and the family will not intervene in society. It's a dialogic relationship of oppression.

Consider another example. A lesbian's brother gets married. His parents are pathologically homophobic. He has manipulated this prejudice all his life to make up for his own feelings of inadequacy in relationship to his sister who, while disparaged within the family, is far more accomplished than he is within the world. He organizes the entire family to travel thousands of miles to his wedding but excludes his sister. No one in the family will say anything about this to him, nor will they call her to see how she feels. Everyone decides that because it is his WEDDING, his heterosexuality makes his feelings more important than hers. That he is human and she is not. And so they collude with excluding her, causing her great pain. If they approached the brother as a group and told him that they would not be manipulated into scapegoating the sister, he would not be able to carry out his plan. But it doesn't occur to them. It's a wedding after all. When the sister tries to read a novel or see a movie or play expressing this experience, there aren't any. If she tries to create one, she is told by the publisher that it's beautifully written but that it is special interest, not for the general public. The arts and entertainment industry—the producers of popular culture—reinforce the cruelty by actively keeping it unrepresented. In this way, the perpetrators remain unaccountable. It's a dynamic system of perpetuation of domination through censorship of human experience.

This multiply reinforced exclusion is powerful and devastating to gay people because it defies the typical private/public dichotomy on which society's safety net depends. Usually the family is a refuge from the cruelties of the culture. Or, if the family is a source of cruelty, the larger society is a refuge from the family. But when the family and the larger society enact the identical structures of exclusion and diminishment, the individual has no place of escape. Especially when the institutions of representation ALSO don't allow the experience and subsequent feelings to be expressed.

Since gay people face false accusations and shunning every day and in every arena of life, our behavior and state of mind can be deeply affected by either withstanding the assaults, or desperately trying to avoid them. Either way the active oppression of shunning and false accusation manipulates and controls gay people's lives to varying degrees. The repetition and ease with which both exclusion and distortion are imposed make it seem regular, daily, and even, in fact, not happening. It becomes "just how things are," a falsely naturalized state, when it is actually designed and imposed by force.

Historically, gay people have tried to protect themselves by retreating into subculture and/or relationships. But even these structures are often not able to resist particularly venomous onslaughts by family and society. Gay subculture in particular is extremely vulnerable to scapegoating—especially when rooted in interlocking difference between genders, races, and classes. The subculture and the romantic relationship itself can therefore become an instrument of the larger structures of cruelty particularly when there is no accountability and no one to be accountable to. As long as no one cares how she is treated, the discarded homosexual becomes a convenient target for the cruelty of others, whether that cruelty is rooted in heterosexual privilege or in other oppressed people's trauma.

I am reminded here of Yvonne Welbon's brilliant short film *Monique*, in which the African American filmmaker tells the story of her first-grade-classroom enemy, Monique. How much they hated each other, how much they hurt each other, how much they displayed their hatred for others to see. Then, at the end of the film, Welbon shows the old group photo from first grade, and we suddenly realize that she and Monique were the only blacks in the class. You see this all the time. Other gay people are encouraged and rewarded by state, family, power cliques—by individuals and institutions—to not identify with each other, to not help each other, to not stand up for each other. And when the betrayals take place, they get rewarded. Whether it's a successful lesbian producer who never develops a lesbian play, gay republicans, a man who violates his lover and receives the approval of his homophobic family for doing so, or a woman who uses the prejudicial courts to deny her lover custody and wins the support of the state. In every case, they extend the hand of scapegoating.

In short, once we can accept that just because one person wants to exclude another, it doesn't give them the right to do so, we have to look at the moral implications of this realization for action. When a family cuts off a child because she is a lesbian, that refusal, that silence, is morally wrong, even though the society and laws endorse it.

We have to understand by extension that when one gay person cuts off his/her lover/friend as a consequence of that person's powerlessness (powerlessness created by her homosexuality), that refusal, that silence is also morally wrong. It is the same action. And when a gay man runs a theater and develops young gay male writers while humiliating and ignoring women, it is an extension of the same action. He does it because he can. Human beings deserve, by virtue of being born, acknowledgment, recognition, interactivity, and negotiation. To deprive people of that because they have no supporting institution insisting on their rights is unjust. To do it to a daughter, sister, lover, or colleague is the same injustice. If one would have to go to a court of law, recite the entire pattern, beginning with the originating action, and show the consequential chain of events, would an unbiased jury be persuaded that to shun this person was justified? Similarly, if we could bring a class-action suit against all of the main-stage theaters in the United States to show cause why there is no lesbian play in the American canon, I assure you that the only reason that would emerge is that there is cultural hegemony among the selectors. That there is no inherently justifiable principle maintaining this exclusion and its conse-quential humiliations and diminishments.

I am trying to articulate, for the first time, the nature and long term consequences of familial homophobia on the gay individual and the broader culture. I am trying to quantify something that is persistent and yet invisible. And then I hope to make overt and conscious the human obligation to enact third party intervention. The purpose of this book is to open up a new category of thought and to explore and discuss, not define, it. To disagree with its precisions is to enter into the dialogue and to finally acknowledge what is already there.

"THE OPPRESSED WILL ALWAYS BELIEVE THE WORST ABOUT THEMSELVES"

—Frantz Fanon

The betrayal of gay people by their heterosexual family members is as effective as it is undeserved. This confusing combination leaves us with a lifetime burden of having to try to come to terms with and understand the experience. One coping mechanism is to pretend that nothing is happening. Many gay people will say that their families are "fine." But when you ask for details, this means, basically, that the gay person has not been completely excluded from family events. Or that their partner, if they have one, is allowed in the house. Very few experience their personhood, lives, and feelings to be actively understood as equal to the heterosexual family members. Often parents or siblings keep the person's homosexuality secret from others, or euphemize it. They vote for politicians who hurt gay people; they contribute to religious organizations that humiliate gay people;

SARAH SCHULMAN

they patronize cultural products that depict gay people as pathological. They speak and act in ways that reinforce the idea of gay people as "special interest." In many ways the message is clear that the gay person is not fully human. But because many gay people know others who have been more severely punished by their family's prejudices, they look on their own continued compromised inclusion to be miraculously positive and a product of their own correct behavior.

Let's face it—most people are average and cannot conceptualize beyond what has already been articulated, especially if it is an official point of view. Gay people are no different. Women are no different. Poor people are no different. I teach in a working-class school, a branch of the City University of New York. About a third of my students are working-class Italian and Irish kids with questionable economic futures. Eighty percent of my students have a friend, acquaintance, or family member who has been in Iraq. Many of these students voted for George Bush twice, and Staten Island was the only borough of New York City to vote for John McCain. I have had many students who supported the war even though they and their friends are the cannon fodder. They vote for politicians who cut funding for the City University while they sit in over-crowded classrooms without adequate course offerings, counseling, financial aid, library, and computer services. They identify with rich people, who they think, got that way because they are smart. Every day I hear them defend people who are hurting them; I see them supporting systems that oppress them. And when their friends and relatives kill and are killed in Iraq, they justify the pain. In our classes together, we discuss this over and over again: where do they get their information? From television, which they watch uncritically.

Many of my students find analysis and critical thinking to be emotionally upsetting. It makes them feel disloyal to their parents and their church and their government. They would rather not know that what is said on television is often not true. The consequences of this knowledge are too disruptive, even if the ignorance keeps them from reaching their life goals of having interesting, financially stable jobs.

For gay people, the same tropes are in place. Many gay people believe that Ellen DeGeneres was the first openly lesbian performer. They don't realize that she achieved success while in the closet and then came out. That if she had in fact been out all along—like comics Marga Gomez or Kate Clinton—she never would have achieved that level of success. They think that Dorothy Allison writes novels with lesbian protagonists, not realizing that if she did, they might never have heard of her or her books. They think that the movies are now representing lesbian characters because Charlize Theron won an Oscar for playing a lesbian murderer and Hilary Swank for playing a queer who was murdered. But they can't find lesbian protagonists in nonpathologized or non-punished roles. Most people don't have the ability to decode these systems, and so they believe they are being represented, being given opportunities to succeed, being rewarded, and having their stories told—even though none of these things are actually happening. This observation is not to minimize the gifts of any of the above individuals, nor to criticize them in any way. Their successes are stupendous personal achievements for them as individuals, but these events do not hold the meaning for lesbian life that they are often mistakenly said to have. In some cases, this recognition is actually a reflection of how oppression operates, not the reverse as is sometimes claimed or thought.

Because gay people are forced to have a high awareness about heterosexual cruelty in order to try to avoid it, we know an enormous amount about the structures and functions of homophobia and about the manifestations of the homophobic variant in a wide spectrum of individual heterosexual types. However, heterosexuals spend almost no time thinking about how their behavior is homophobic, what its impact is on the society and, most importantly, they do not consider its impact on us personally. They retain a false sense of supremacy by not being accountable. Not thinking is one of their privileges. After all, in every system of domination, the dominant group knows only about themselves, while the members of the subordinate group know about their own lives as well as the lives of the dominant group members. So, those with the most power have the least information about how other people live. If straight people were forced to think about and be accountable for their behavior toward us, they would have to justify their actions. And that would be pretty hard to do.

In order for us to come to a cultural agreement that homophobia within the family is wrong, we need one basic shared assumption: homophobia is not the fault of gay people. Homophobia is not caused by gay people. There is nothing that a gay person can ever do to justify it. Homophobia is a pathological manifestation of heterosexual culture. As a pure prejudice, it is wrong and as social currency within and outside of the family, it is despicable. If a straight person does not like a gay person or is competing with a gay person, whether in the marketplace or in sibling rivalry, it is never appropriate to use homophobia as a leveler.

The manifestations of familial homophobia can take many forms:

- Some families entirely and thoroughly exclude gay and lesbian members through outright ban.
- Some allow them a partial participation provided that the person never shows or discusses his or her own life.

- Some allow a lover to be present as long as that person is not fully acknowledged in his or her actual role.
- Some allow full physical participation by the gay person and their lover but constantly enforce a clear message that they are not as important as the heterosexuals in the family and/or that their relationship is lesser than heterosexual relationships or the consequence of pathology.
- Some rely on repeated humiliations and diminishments.
- Some enforce the above with more degrees of subtlety.

None of these possibilities are acceptable or reasonable. All have long-term destructive effects on the gay person as their diminishment is regularly reinforced. That gay people have to tolerate this or be complicit with it in order to be loved is very distorting. And many of these diminishments are played out later by gay people on each other. All of these options have long term destructive effects on the lives of homosexuals within the family because they reinforce the heterosexuals' own investment in homophobia. In the end, the family is the training ground and model for other social institutions in which homosexuals are expected to acquiesce.

Familial homophobia begins at the beginning of the gay

family member's life. It usually starts as a false set of standards by which the gay person's behaviors and emotions are pathologized. That is, things that are good and true about them are treated as bad and wrong. The gay person has a number of possible reactions to this pathologization, all of which are ultimately punishing and destructive to their lives:

- They can obscure their homosexuality in order to avoid being punished when they have done nothing wrong, but this is a brutal form of punishment in itself.
- They can continue to behave as though nothing is happening, while being consistently subjected to diminishment.
- They can object to the distorted behavior of the homophobes in question.

Unfortunately, this last option, which is the most appropriate response, is the one that will ultimately cause them the most punishment. Homophobia as a system does not tolerate opposition. Gay people are expected to capitulate. And to be grateful for crumbs. When they are not, it is seen as even more of an example of how troubled they are, how mentally ill, how maladjusted, bad, angry, and wrong. When the originating action of homophobia has the consequence of making them angry or upset, they then get blamed for being angry or upset and that result gets repositioned as the justification or cause for their oppression. The more they take the noble, responsible, and mature action of resisting homophobia, the more they are viewed as troublesome, inappropriate, and detrimental.

The reason that the existence of homophobia and the practice of homophobes are able to render good, honest, caring, productive, dignified people as pathological is because homophobia itself is the pathology. It is an anti-social condition that causes violence and destroys families. It not only makes society punish and exclude people, but it punishes these same people for trying to restore the larger society to sanity. The perpetrators, who are the destructive ones, are described as the neutral standard of behavior, while the people, who are not only victimized but have the decency to fight back (which is the most beautiful model of social responsibility), are described as expendable and undesirable. The final ironic twist is that whenever a situation does arise in which homophobia is pointed to as being socially destructive or personally wrong, the homophobe tends to actually blame his own behavior on gay people themselves. And there are always gay people willing to point the same finger, gay people who have been persuaded that tolerating or being complicit with prejudice in order to be "loved" is love.

I believe in, am committed to, and am working toward a cultural agreement that homophobia is a social pathology and that society's best interest is served by any program or practice that mitigates homophobia. The family is the best place to start because the family is where people first learn its power. That is why the commitment to eradicating homophobia must begin with the family.

The model I have in mind for the social transformation to a consensus that homophobia is a social pathology comes from feminism and how the conceptualization of rape was transformed in the 1970s and 1980s in the United States and subsequently globally. While this is still a rape culture, while most rape still goes unpunished, while many men feel that rape is a privilege and a right, while rape is still a form of entertainment and a strategy of war, there has been a broad transformation in cultural consensus. Rape is now *officially* wrong. The practice of rape is more pathologized and victims of rape are less stigmatized. There is a legal consensus that rape is wrong. Women are not blamed for being raped with the regularity that we once were. In other words, there is broad cultural agreement that rape is wrong, and this agreement was achieved by a social movement rooted in human experience. This can be an instructive model for the transformation of social codes around familial homophobia. While we can't always change people's actions or their beliefs, we can change the cultural consensus, which in turn can both influence some people's actions and transform their beliefs while providing more support for victims to resist.

The reality is that people with power can never be persuaded to give it up, but they can be forced. Through the creation of a critical mass (a significant sector of the society amassing power for their constituency), certain social transformations can be kick-started or advanced. In this way, by creating a counter-cultural option for social behavior, social change has a chance.

After all, forty years ago if people heard a neighbor being beaten by her husband, they were far less likely to intervene or call the police. It was viewed as a private family matter by both the state and civilians. Now, people know that they are supposed to call the police, and inherent in that understanding is the belief that the police are supposed to pathologize and interrupt this behavior. This is an enormous cultural transformation. It means that, regarding domestic violence, there is now an authority recognized that is larger than the patriarchal family. The same transformation can occur within the realm of familial homophobia. Both for victims and for perpetrators.

CULTURAL CRISIS,
NOT PERSONAL PROBLEM

Familial homophobia is something that gay people discuss with each other with a regular, daily urgency. And yet it has not made it into the official public discourse. In some ways, it is our most important story and so it is worth trying to understand why it has remained a secret. Emotionally, the pain is often unbearable, inarticulable, and the solution eludes us. We often speak about it to each other in shorthand. One gay person can meet another in an elevator, make a passing quip about his family, and be perfectly understood. And we also blame each other for it. As distorted as it is for gay people to blame each other for straight people's homophobia, this common projection shows how embedded this conversation is in our relationships with each other.

On the other hand, dear, close straight friends who have known gay people for years may never be able to fully comprehend the dimensions and impact of the homophobia that their close gay friends face from their families. The gulf in experience is so profound and has so much specificity that its full impact can feel impossible to convey. After all, straight people also have problems with their families and so often cannot differentiate between the degree. It's the old "white people have problems too" syndrome, in which the dominant person is unable to imagine the burden of prejudice on top of regular human difficulties.

Why begin with the family? In many ways, we can now understand this force we have previously called "society" to actually be the collective interaction of our families. Regarding homosexuality, the word "society" has become a euphemism for our families. Whereas this was always true, albeit unconsciously, now that so many families are aware that they have gay or lesbian members, the family is increasingly the *overt* building block of homophobia. At this point in cultural awareness, any family in which the alienated, scapegoated party is also the gay party, must interrogate the relationship between the two conditions. How can it be that the only black person in the office is the only person everyone hates? I think it is safe to say that in any family where the only gay person is the alienated person, there is homophobia.

Being heard in opposition to this construction is very difficult because the more integrity queer people have about their homosexuality, the less access they have to mainstream discourse. A very extreme but entertaining example has to do with the exclusion and scapegoating of gay people by Barack Obama during his campaign and in the early days of his presidency. Despite his support for gay marriage in 1996, candidate Obama asserted during the election that "marriage is ordained by God to be between one man and one woman." Then Rick Warren, the anti-gay, anti-abortion evangelical, was chosen by President Obama to publicly pray at the constitutionally secular but actually Christian inauguration. Warren was interviewed on the television show *Dateline* by reporter Ann Curry about the fact that his Saddleback Church excludes gays and lesbians from membership. "Our church has done more for people with AIDS than any other church," said Warren. "Oh, yes," Curry concurred, "And gay people say that, they love you for it." Of course, gay people were excluded from this mainstream televised conversation and so the two of them continued to lie without refute. Some days later, Melissa Etheridge, a singer who became famous while in the closet and only then came out as a lesbian who publicly married but donated no money to fight Proposition 8 (the anti-gay ballot measure in California), met with Warren and stated publicly that he is "not a gay hater." Regardless of how you feel about Etheridge's music, someone who was in the closet until she was famous is not the person who should be deciding the standard of behavior that benefits lesbian, gay, bisexual, and transgender (LGBT) peo-

ple. The situation with Rick Warren is a classic case of someone very powerful seeing himself as compassionate when in
fact he is destructive and then is reinforced by the most gay
people's lack of access to media and their replacement by gay
people with histories of self-oppression. The exclusion of
LGBT people from the Obama family became uncon-
testable because the people who could speak to it truthfully
were marginalized. Instead gay and lesbian people became
dependent on straight people who have privileges we don't
have, like Frank Rich, to take Obama and Warren to task.
The president then went on to use the words "straight and
gay" in his inauguration speech while appointing no openly
gay people to his cabinet. In the end, the straight "pro-gay"
commentators are morally elevated; Obama and Warren's
anti-gay exclusion is fulfilled; and LGBT people are kicked
out of the family, while some of us are explaining to each
other that what is happening isn't really happening.

I use the word "family" here to define cultural construc-
tions of belonging because the family is the place where
most people are first instructed in homophobia. The family is
where most gay people experience homophobia for the first
time. It is the model for social exclusion, for it is also where
most straight people learn to use homophobia to elevate
themselves within the family politic, which is the prototype
for the broader social politic.

As in the replication of many social dynamics, homophobia originates and is enforced, initially, within the family. This has made family relationships into the primary source of pain and diminishment in the lives of many gay people. We pay an enormously debilitating price for familial homophobia at the same time that heterosexuals within the family learn how to (and have the choice to) use it as currency. And yet the perpetuation of homophobic practice is repeatedly blamed on gay people themselves. We are depicted as being inherently deserving of punishment, even though, in actuality, we have not done anything wrong. After all, homophobia is exclusively a product of heterosexual culture. It is not caused by homosexuals or by gay culture.

Sadly, this paradigm confuses gay people ourselves. Conversely, when we insist on inclusion, full recognition, and access to process, we can get internally pathologized as "militants," "activists," and "stalkers," even by each other. The dangerous exclusion is naturalized as benign and the desire for accountability is falsely seen as a threat when it is really life enhancing. To this day, productive individual actions and group efforts that make positive contributions to the culture are still seen as compromising the right to exclude. I recently had a conversation with a young Asian gay male who had graduated from Yale. He was probably born in 1983. He told me, "I have mixed feelings about ACT UP, those confrontational tactics turn people off." Of course, he is alive today because of ACT UP. Similarly, I was told by Jeremy, a gay man who works at a theater that has never produced a lesbian play, that my desire to have them produce lesbian plays is "too intense." When I asked him if he thought that Tony Kushner might be intense if his points of view were systematically censored, he did not respond. The basic desire to be acknowledged and included is seen as pathological, while the destructive exclusion of people's lives becomes the definition of reasonable.

Familial homophobia exists with force and brutality in every ethnic, class, racial, and religious group. The modes of manifestation may be different, but it is always there. So for example, a working-class black rural family can be as devastating in its homophobia as an upper-class suburban white family. A liberal middle-class Jewish family in New York can be as fiercely rejecting as a blue-collar Mennonite farming family in Pennsylvania. A born-again Christian family in Iowa is just as capable of being strong enough to love their gay children as a lefty academic family in Boston. And a white Unitarian feminist theorist in London is just as capable of being homophobic to her gay sister as a South Asian dentist in Detroit. It is really about individual strength of character and the family's capacity for love.

The capacity for feeling, strong enough to overwhelm social expectation, is at the root of the homosexual identity. This transgression is what coming-out is all about. Without having experienced the coming-out process themselves, straight people often do not have a model for such a fierce level of resistance.

The emotional deprivation of familial homophobia is not as easily accessible to potential straight allies. Inherent in this problem of comprehension is that people who are allowed into their families view many aspects of inclusion in family life as neutral or even as a burden instead of as a privilege. Because they are not aware of these privileges, they can't understand the loss of them.

At the same time, the perpetrators often misconstrue the exclusion as their "right." Throughout the history of cruelty to gay people, exclusion has consistently been theorized as a natural unquestioned option. Legally, straight people have long argued that it is their right to not have to rent apartments, give jobs, or serve meals to gay people if they don't want to. In the 2008 election, Barack Obama, Hillary Clinton, John McCain, and Sarah Palin all united around their shared belief that gays and lesbians should be excluded from certain legal rights and protections. There was little questioning of this consensus for exclusion. Similarly, families exclude and shun gay members without anyone questioning their behavior. And gay people ourselves take advantage of the lack of inclusion to exclude partners from emotional and material processes that straight people can access through social and legal institutions. There is a consistent model of shunning across the board that implies—in the end—that no one has to be accountable for their negative actions toward gay and lesbian people.

And of course our straight friends may be compromised by their own behavior within their own families toward their own gay family members. After all, one of the most pervasive uses of homophobia within a family is by family members who actually have no inherent prejudices toward gay people but manipulate their family's prejudices to achieve greater currency internally. It's like the folks who didn't really care about Communism but denounced others to the blacklist to win promotion in their fields. They exploit prejudicial systems for their own advancement, even if they are not ideologically committed to those systems. In this confused way, straight people may have gay friends while participating in creating their gay relatives as second-class family members. As someone who has a lot of straight friends, I am no longer surprised to see how many of them allow gay family members to be marginalized, regardless of how progressive they may be. When it comes to their own privileges on the job, in their family, or in the Obama administration, they just don't want to risk losing currency. What I've learned from this, strangely, is that having close personal authentic relationships with gay people may have no impact on whether or not a straight person exploits homophobia in his or her family or other currency circles. Although this seems nonsensical emotionally, our current social structure encourages it by providing no consequence for this kind of duplicitous behavior. Although theoretically it sounds ridiculous, in applied real life terms it's much easier to love gay people and not stand up for them than to risk your own privileges to have a consistent trajectory of behavior. And this applies to gay people ourselves. We too can betray each other, shun and exclude each other, with more reward than negative consequence.

I have heard straight friends tell me that they have a relative who is gay, or is thought to be gay, who is ostracized or demeaned inside their family. But they don't think about interrupting the process. When I ask them why, they are often surprised. It was never considered to be a possibility. Never have I found friends in this position who had already thoroughly considered their responsibility to intervene. Often they project that the gay person doesn't want to be offered help. Or they justify and excuse their inaction based on the feelings of discomfort that arise when they consider diminishing their own precariously established relationships with other family members. Not wanting to feel what their gay family member feels is enough to excuse their own inaction. It's a clear message that one person's just treatment can be easily sacrificed for the comfort of another.

Most social movements have been constructed by people who were related: civil rights and labor movements involve multi-generations of rebellion by the same families. Even feminism has tried to be a movement of mothers and daughters. But the gay and lesbian movement, like the disability movement, is made up of people who stand apart from the fate of their family members, and whose most intense oppression experiences may be at the hand of those same relatives. Since most people do not have a capacity for justice strong enough to overcome social expectation, it makes more sense for us to point to social expectation as the proposed site for transformation, rather than on individual heterosexuals and their capacity for original thought.

Unfortunately, without third-party intervention, we each often still are brainwashed into conceptualizing of familial homophobia as our own individual problem. We see it within the specificities of our own families, and we often have to enter those families alone and deal with this problem alone. We can commiserate with others later, but the battle is ours alone. This false privatization of familial homophobia has kept us from acknowledging that it is not a personal problem, but rather a cultural crisis. A change in attitude necessary for this acknowledgment would have many consequences for action.

First, it would mean that transforming standards for how gay people are treated in families would become a public demand of our public political agenda. While we demand changes in material conditions like

- employment protection
- cultural representation, and
- integrating into the larger community as openly gay people

we would also be publicly articulating and demanding changes in how we are treated by our families.

There is some precedence for this, after all, in the feminist movement of the 1970s, which addressed behavior, values, and speech within what is falsely conceptualized of as "the private sphere." It politicized women's role and experience in the family and undid the false "naturalization" of social structures that keep women from power.

The second and more important consequence of making familial homophobia a public matter and not a private one is that we would not each be fighting it alone. We would be fighting it together, in the same way that we have faced the AIDS crisis and many other public, communal crises. We would have organizations, events, books, public forums, debates on television, education—all of the tools that we have used in the past to bring a subject out of the shadows and onto the American dinner table adapted of course to the new technologies. Organizations like PFLAG (Parents and Friends of Lesbians and Gays) could be much more effective in publicly stigmatizing homophobia and normalizing homosexuality within the family structure.

In the homophobic family, the logic of good and evil is primordially distorted. There, heterosexuality is awarded and homosexuality is punished, even though there is nothing wrong with homosexuality and nothing right with heterosexuality. The punishment of the homosexual family member has no justification and yet is a primary assumption of heterosexual society. Restated more simply: most people do what they're told, so tell them something different. Change the social standard of how gay people are supposed to be treated and most people will change their behavior to follow.

If we really believe that homophobia is wrong, we must act that way. Any vision of real justice for gay people must include an understanding that the homophobic family is inherently a corrupt structure *because* of its homophobia and should not be privileged. The irony is that it pretends that it is neutral, objective, normal, right, and value free, the opposite of its actual social function. In other words, as long as the family is a homophobic institution, the nuclear, extended, birth or adopted, inter-generational family is not a valid institution and should be stripped of its authority. Ironically, the homophobic family lies at the heart of what we are told is the model for loyalty, caring, love, and identity. If the weight of subjectivity could be shifted from this false paradigm, then the ability of the homophobic family to claim goodness would be diminished.

The logical conclusion of such a twist in values would be a general acknowledgment that if people cannot fully love, support, respect, and most importantly, defend and protect their gay or lesbian child, they should not be parents. If they cannot give up their privileges to fully stand with their gay or lesbian siblings or parents, they should lose social approval. In other words, I'm imagining a transformed social value in which homophobia is the action worthy of punishment and exclusion, not homosexuality. Where shunning is punished and resolution praised.

This statement is both supremely reasonable and yet completely without social context because a standard of ethics regarding homophobia in the family has not yet been articulated. Instead of focusing on the homophobia as the subject of inquiry, the great distortion has been to interrogate the origins of homosexuality. Today there is a national obsession with proving that homosexuality is one thing with one "cause," which liberals believe is rooted in a biological deficiency or abnormality and Christians believe is rooted in "choice" and subject to conversion. In order to develop a vision of how to eradicate homophobia within the family, we must reject completely any framework that maintains homosexuality as a category of deviance that needs to be explained and instead focus entirely on the origins of and solutions to homophobia. This means focusing on the perpetrators, their motives, consciousness, and actions with the purpose of creating deterrents necessary for gay people to have healthier emotional lives.

HOMOPHOBIA AS A PLEASURE SYSTEM

Many natural and unavoidable mistakes have been made as the gay liberation movement tried to first grasp, then understand, then convey the system of cruelty by heterosexuals toward homosexuals. The nature of this cruelty is hard to initially conceptualize because it is simultaneously pervasive, invisible, and deeply painful. The people who are doing it often don't know that they are doing it or pretend that they do not. The repetition and the dailiness make it seem normal. It is very difficult to try to imagine a life without this constant diminishment. And the depths of its consequences, coupled with its total lack of justification, are alienating to fully realize. The reinscription of these cruelties within our own trusting, loving relationships are difficult to articulate because there is no place to do so.

When reviewing our errors of understatement, they seem innocent, childlike. How sad that so many of our oversimplifications were caused by our love and trust of other human beings and our consequent inability to understand how they could be so ruthless in exploiting their advantages over us.

Why, after all, try to explain what exclusion and punishment feel like, and why they are wrong? Somewhere in the choice to communicate lies a profound optimism and pure belief that people don't want to do evil, and if they realize what they are doing, they will stop it. That fundamentally people are cruel only because they do not know that this is what they are doing. If they had awareness, they would choose otherwise. That cruelty happens by accident.

Most gay people were born into a family. Usually the parent(s) were heterosexual or appeared to be so. This creates, immediately, the bizarre construction of a closed living system in which the parents enjoy rights (legal, social, and the rights of self-perception) that one or more of their children will never enjoy. We love our parents no matter what. And most parents begin with the best of intentions. And yet the system of supremacy into which straight people are inaugurated is so persuasive, so dominant in its invisibility, and therefore unidentifiable, that parents and siblings and other relatives are often not individual enough to transcend its inherent cruelties. Instead they reinforce them to greater and lesser extents, and because we love our parents, we make excuses or try to help them expand their thinking, often without fully acknowledging the impact of their prejudices on our emotional lives. The greatest of which is to continue their dirty work in our treatment of each other.

All of this converges on the question of VISIBILITY. Visibility was a construct that the gay and lesbian movement invented to explain and excuse the cruelty we were experiencing. We denied that it was intentional. Instead we invented the idea that it was an inadvertent consequence of heterosexuals having a lack of information about what we are really like. If they would discover how we truly are, they would not want to hurt us. And since they were doing everything imaginable—using every social institution to make it impossible for us to be truly seen—we would have to subject ourselves to extreme violation in order to force a cathartic experience for them that would make them better. This process required shock troops of certain stupendously courageous gay and lesbian individuals to "come out" and be fully subjected to the force of punishment, thereby creating the inevitable social change that we felt would accompany recognition. Some of us forced them to see us, expecting that once they would see us, they would love us, and then realize that our disenfranchisement was morally wrong, and they would then join with us in correcting these structures of exclusion, both emotional and social. The plan was that the vanguard homosexuals, willing to take the punishment, would then make things easier for other, less courageous ones looking on from the wings waiting for this battle to achieve a more equitable field. These others could then enter the process with progressively fewer degrees of loss, but filled with recognition for their brave predecessors, and what we had done for them. Looking back at the way we created the issue of "visibility" as a strategy for change is a painful confrontation with the realization that it was an engagement with magical thinking.

We believed that straight people hate and hurt us because they don't know us. If we could have visibility, they would realize that we are fine and would accept us. This theory has been disproven by history. Now we have enormous visibility and the hatred and overt campaigns against us ranging from commodification to constitutional amendments to dehumanizingly false representations in popular culture have intensified and become more deliberate. Clearly ignorance was not the determining factor in what caused homophobia. There is much more volition on the part of homophobes than we ever imagined.

A second, concurrent theory that we relied on for many years was the idea that heterosexuals experience a "fear" of homosexuals. This was the famous "phobia." We fantasized that it was rooted both in ignorance but also in some insecurity about their own heterosexuality. Whenever extremely violent behavior emerges, this theory is trotted out again. Repeatedly our proposal is used against us and reshaped so that gay-bashers become repressed homosexuals who cannot accept their own identity. This variation on the "black-on-black crime" theory, in which white people have no role, positions our oppressors as other, unself-acknowledged homosexuals, while the heterosexual majority remains innocent and not responsible.

It seems obvious, at this point, that neither of these explanations is sufficient. Knowledge of and about homosexuals does not dilute homophobia; it only pushes it into more virulent and in some cases more sophisticated modes of containment and justification.

Simultaneously, it is clear that the people who benefit from these configurations are not "hidden" homosexuals but rather the heterosexual majority. What is most difficult to face, but increasingly obvious as gay visibility provokes containment, but not equality, is that homophobes enjoy feeling superior, rely on the pleasure of enacting their superiority, and go out of their way to resist change that would deflate their sense of supremacy. Homophobia makes heterosexuals feel better about themselves. It's not fear—it's fun.

We know from photographs of happy picnicking white families laughing underneath the swinging body of a tortured, lynched black man, or giggly white U.S. soldiers leading naked Iraqis on leashes, or terrified humiliated Jews surrounded by laughing smiling Nazis that human beings love being cruel. They enjoy the power, and go far beyond social expectation to carry out the kind of cruelty that makes them feel bigger. In short, homophobia is not a phobia at all. It is a pleasure system.

On the surface, there are lessons to be learned by theories of totalitarianism developed by other groups in other historical moments that resonate with our condition. Most deceptively appealing is the popularized version of Hannah Arendt's observation of the "banality of evil." Translated to our condition, this would be an understanding that people are homophobic because they are expected to be. That there is a great deal of conformity involved in the practice, and it is not exceptional. The common understanding of this idea is that people are homophobic because they have been told to be and are trained to be. As a result, they become so fearful of the repercussions of dissension that they cannot act independently. They are being controlled by a broad, yet invisible, social force. Their own need for approval and the material privileges that approval accompanies, supersedes their love and acceptance of their family members and their sense of justice. In many ways, this is an appealing theory. It separates homophobia from the individuals who enact it. It implies that the great social punishment that awaits detractors is so menacing that they will do anything to avoid it. After all, we know what homophobia feels like and can sympathize with straight people's desire to avoid its consequences at all costs. Most interestingly, at the basis of this analysis is the recognition, though usually unarticulated, that to dissolve homophobia in the family means that straight people would lose things that they now have. However, that process is more complex than we have previously understood.

While it is true that if straight people wish to join the fight to end homophobia, they must give up certain material privileges in the interim, the losses to them are actually more long term than we have previously understood. For the time being, I believe that the most ethical position for straight people, in the age of homophobia, is to relinquish all their privileges until we have them too. It is the sexuality version of boycotting grapes. If a critical mass of straight people withdraw from discriminatory social institutions until they are available to gay people, those institutions will cease to have social currency. They will not be able to function until homophobia is eradicated. If a gay person is not allowed to babysit a same-sex niece or nephew, then the straight people in the family should refuse to do so as well. The deprivation of resources will force the homophobes, in most cases, to re-assess their behavior or be alienated.

But this protest fantasy has been conceptualized as a temporary condition while it is actually a permanent one. Implicit in this vision is the understanding that once the homophobic behavior has been removed, everything can get back to normal. If, to give a benign example, homophobic Uncle Arthur organizes Christmas dinner around the schedules of the heterosexual couples in the family and the homosexual partner's schedule is not considered, then no one should participate in Christmas dinner. Since the originating Arthur may decide that something is better than nothing, the social consensus created by the other straight family members will force the homosexual partner's needs to be fully and equally considered. Of course, for this to be organized currently depends on the gay members actively agitating for supportive action on the part of straights. But if there were a broad cultural agreement that heterosexual non-participation was the expected mode of behavior, the burden would be off the individual gay people in the family.

But what about once the accommodation is made? Then what happens? Can everyone live happily ever after, with the gay people having the same access as the straights? Probably not. Here's why.

On the bulletin board at The Jerusalem Women's Center, I noticed a posted saying clipped from a magazine: "Equality is not when the female Einstein gets promoted to Assistant Professor, but when female mediocrities can climb as quickly as male mediocrities." I thought long and hard about this statement. The first part is recognizable, familiar to any woman of outstanding ability or accomplishment. But the second part increasingly disturbed me. If male mediocrities can move forward, how can female mediocrities join them? By definition, the rapid rise of mediocre men means that caste, not ability, is the measure. Their presence in positions of authority and power are stand-ins for other people of greater ability whose caste profile excludes them from access. It would be technically impossible for female mediocrities to rise as long as male mediocrities still hold the power. There are just a limited number of places.

Inherent in this conundrum is one of the fundamental problems that keep us from honestly facing the phenomenon of familial homophobia. This is the problem of a false discourse of tolerance. This discourse states that people who have been unfairly excluded from fully expressing themselves, fully participating in their families, i.e., their societies, can be painlessly included without anyone else's position having to be adjusted.

The truth, however, is that there will never be equality for women until male mediocrities can no longer rise. Women of ability will be able to take their rightful spot only when mediocre men are removed from power. If success means opportunity at one's level of merit, those now falsely inflated would be removed from the category of "successful." This necessary equation, one that no one wants to admit to, reveals the frightening truth. Oppressed people, people unfairly excluded from full participation, cannot have their rightful place until the people who exclude them experience a diminishment of their own access and power. No matter how much we pretend otherwise, one cannot happen without the other.

Similarly, gay people will never have a full and fair place in the family structure until straight people have less currency, less entitlement, and less power than they currently hold. In other words, until the family structure is re-imagined to serve gay people more, and thereby, service straight people less. To pretend that straight people can keep all their advantages while gay people can be allowed to access them is preposterous. Gay people's exclusion is predicated on straight people's privileges. Only if they have fewer privileges will there be less exclusion.

So what is in it for them?

Nothing.

As history has shown us, when black people can sit in the front of the bus, more white people have to stand. When jobs open up for women, they become more competitive for men. In the attempt to shift from a caste-based system of privilege and access to a democratic family, social world, and workplace, opportunity becomes increasingly based on merit, ability, and appropriateness and less on gender, race, or sexuality. So, people whose power resides in oppressive systems get demoted. Once we understand that process, we can have a clearer idea of what is at stake in familial homophobia and what will change by dismantling it.

Homophobia in the family functions along the lines of traditional forms of scapegoating. There is currency. It can be emotional, in particular familial approval, love, and interest. It can also be material and financial across a broad spectrum of classes and economic situations. If your brother gives your lover a pair of socks for Christmas, that is one less pair of socks you will have to buy. If your cousin invites you for Thanksgiving dinner, that is one Thanksgiving dinner you won't have to pay for. But for many of us the emotional support and love that a family can provide can have a much higher value than any possible financial support they can provide. And conversely, not being allowed to return love, to participate in family decisions, to care for children, etc., is accompanied by a high emotional cost. Monetarily, if your family has the resources but refuses to lend you money for an emergency because they have pathologized you, then the currency can actually mean the difference between life and death, home and homelessness, education and underdevelopment, safety and danger, food and starvation.

In other words, homophobia within a family means that some members will experience emotional and material deprivation because they are homosexual. Or because the gay person manifests consequences of the other's originating homophobic behavior, which implicates the homophobe and inspires a retaliatory smoke screen of false accusation; for example, "It's not because you're gay, it's because you're angry." But not asking, *why* are you angry? Frankly, I often find that the myth of the angry lesbian/angry woman/angry black man is really the rage of the dominant culture person at being asked to look at themselves. They are so furious that they see other people's productive positive actions for change as threatening. Regardless of who they really are in the world, whether or not they are socially contributive or parasitic, within the family the heterosexuals are higher for one reason only—they are straight. Many people unconsciously rely on this elevation based on heterosexuality, marriage, and parenthood to feel comfortable and loved. If the contrast was not there with homosexual family members and these were not the grounds for love and approval, they would be in the same boat within the family that they are in the larger social world. It is a desperate need that cannot be filled by anything else in life. Why would straight people ever give it up?

Understanding what is at stake for them makes participation in familial homophobia far less benign than a simple conformity or blind imitation. Given that the rewards for heterosexuality within the family are so great, it is far more likely that the ways in which each straight person enacts, profits from, and replicates homophobia within the family are proactive. Each person makes decisions, on some level, about which forms of homophobia to participate in, which forms to instigate, which forms are too dramatic. They are constantly selecting and deciding.

As we look for a more sophisticated and realistic assessment of the functions and construction of homophobia, I recommend the work of Dr. Martin Kantor, a psychiatrist and the author of *Homophobia: Description, Development and Dynamics of Gay Bashing* (Praeger, 1998). Dr. Kantor clearly articulates the selection process involved in the implementation of homophobia and the deliberate choice of tactics to achieve self-elevation by diminishing the gay person:

Homophobes abuse gays and lesbians for different reasons in different ways and to different degrees, each reflecting underlying personality problems. . . . Homophobes with a psychopathic antisocial personality disorder bash gays and lesbians for personal gain. . . . Psychopathic homophobes are guiltless people who shamelessly externalize blame so that they can get the good things to which they feel entitled. . . . They can diminish the standing of others to increase their chances of getting something . . . and being manipulative by nature they know how to cleverly excuse their gay bashing with various tricks of logic, to convince themselves and others that their mission is admirable. . . . Perversely dependant homophobes even want their victims to love them. . . . Sadistic homophobes prosper and thrive best when their competition is wounded and crippled. . . . Passive aggressive homophobes withhold. . . . They remain unavailable in time of need. . . . Passive aggressives install glass ceilings. . . . This rational, subtle and indirect hostility is actually the most dangerous and destructive kind because it is the most difficult to identify. . . . Narcissism gives homophobes the sense of self-importance they need to feel comfortable and personally entitled. . . . It helps them suppress their own often considerable and considerably obvious defects. Feeling superior to their victims, they can proceed to persecute them comfortably and without qualms.

For example, if a married woman leaves her husband for a woman, she, her siblings, parents, and any of her grown children have a number of choices as to how to express their homophobia. They can pathologize and distance; they can be violent. They can bring in the state and attempt to have the minor children taken away, as Sharon Bottoms's mother did in Virginia. All of these actions, designed to punish the woman for being gay, elevate the heterosexuals within the family politic. They choose which degree of cruelty they will enact. It is a selection process. Now, no matter what else is wrong with them or their lives, they have one thing that is supreme for certain. They're straight. And their actions, in conjunction with the actions of their other family members, underline that they are good and right for being straight, whereas Sharon Bottoms is wrong and unfit for being gay. How do they select which punitive action to take? These are not acts of blind following. They involve consciousness, awareness, and agency.

In making the transition from understanding homophobia as a blindly passive state of being to seeing it as a strategized, customized series of decisions, it is interesting to go to Daniel Goldhagen's book *Hitler's Willing Executioners* to examine his argument toward an understanding of German volition in the carrying out of the Holocaust. Goldhagen asks some very pertinent questions that can easily be applied to trying to determine the nature of homophobic collaboration within the family:

Would they be punished if they resisted?

They would be punished in that they would lose certain privileges. But their level of punishment would never exceed what the gay family member experiences in their daily life.

Are they being blindly obedient?

While totalitarian systems do blunt people's moral sensibilities, as we have shown above, by exhibiting the power of selection they clearly do not accept all oppressive tasks as necessary.

Do they not fully comprehend the consequences of their actions on their victims?

While there is a callow disregard for the gay person and the impact of homophobia's long-term consequences on their lives, the straight person usually has some access to information about the consequences of their actions. This is information they have to choose not to engage.

Do they feel conflicted about their behavior?

Some may feel guilty but need the benefits. Others may experience their behavior as neutral, objective, and non-existent. But once they become aware that such a thing as homophobia exists, they have to choose to not measure their own behavior by its standard definitions.

Goldhagen's ideas about totalitarian behavior and the fascist personality remind us that all people have the option to judge and act ethically. That there are individuals in all situations who do take responsibility proves the availability of moral behavior as a possibility for the others. There were always white people who opposed slavery, always German Christians who opposed Fascism. There are always Jews who oppose the Israeli occupation, always Americans who oppose the war with Iraq, always men who work for abortion rights. There were always capitalists who opposed the persecution of American Communists and Russian Communists who opposed the persecution of Jews.

Are homophobic family members evil? Well, not if you believe that evil does not have a human face. Yes, the people who won't take responsibility for their dying gay son, won't invite their lesbian sister to their wedding, won't allow their gay cousin to hold their child, won't praise their gay co-worker, won't send their gay son a birthday card, vote for anti-gay politicians, give money to a homophobic church, love films that diminish gay people—those people may have all kinds of great attributes. You may love them. They may have taken you fishing when you were six or made you a quilt for Christmas or had a great sense of humor or looked just like you. That is what evil looks like. Evil knows great old songs, can be weak and vulnerable, can love you, can feed the hungry, can pick out a book because they were thinking of you. Evil can have Alzheimer's. Familial homophobia is deeply human, as all evil is the product of human imagination.

There is also a generational translation of homophobia that changes its face but comes from the same impetus. Whereas your grandparents may have thought you would burn in hell, your parents may have called you once a month but refused to allow your lover in their home. Your sister may let you and your lover come over for Thanksgiving but not let you be alone with her children. It becomes more flexible, more accommodating, perhaps, as the generational context changes, but it is the same animal. A forty-year-old woman living in New York City today probably cannot tell her friends, or herself, that she hates her brother because he's gay. Nor can she tell them that she is cruel to him because her parents hate that he is gay, and this gives her more attention from her parents. Instead, she'll just find another reason that is more generationally suitable. As one straight colleague on a job told me, "It's not your homosexuality that I hate. It's your clothes."

THE FAILURE OF
THERAPEUTIC SOLUTIONS

When a society is not willing to confront the consequences of its cruelty in public, our contemporary culture offers privatized therapy as the only realm where its consequences might be addressed. For gay people, whose needs are not acknowledged, this makes therapy a hugely influential apparatus.

Of course what goes on in the subculture of feminist and gay therapy cannot be known and measured. It can only be experienced. I have experienced a wide variety of dominant cultural therapists as well as gay and feminist therapists, and I have been on the receiving end of other people's behaviors that were encouraged by the whole range of therapists. I am fluent in the experiential culture of these therapies in New York City, and my observations come from those lived experiences.

In my experience, both mainstream as well as feminist and gay therapy has been woefully unsuccessful in addressing familial homophobia and its consequences. Regarding the family itself, the primary strategy of therapists has been to advise gay people to separate from their abusive families and to "create" their own gay families. This is a message I have heard repeatedly for many, many years. In fact, I cannot recall a single therapist who suggested otherwise. However, creating another family is a very risky business. The end result of such an approach is, too often, that the gay person doesn't have a family and the homophobic family remains unstigmatized by their abusive behavior. We lose, and they win.

I personally have had five different therapeutic opportunities for practitioners to intervene with my family's homophobia and/or to model to my family that homophobia is wrong.

- In 1975 when my father caught sixteen-year-old me with my lover, he humiliated me in front of my brother and sister and put the shunning process into effect. I went to my high school guidance counselor and told him what was happening to me. He said, "Don't tell the other students or they will shun you." (It was the first time I heard that word in this context.) What he should have done was practice third-party intervention by calling my parents into school to tell them that what they were doing was wrong. The problem was the absence of social agreement that humiliating your child for being gay was wrong. Even though it was.

- When I was in my twenties, I went to the one gay person who my parents knew, an older man who was a therapist. They claimed he was a friend of theirs. I made an appointment, went to his office, told him what I was being subjected to, and he told me to never speak to them again.

    Neither of these people felt that I had a right to have a family. And neither of them was willing to make my family uncomfortable with their behavior. They wanted me to have all the information and all the burden.

- In my early thirties, I asked my father to come with me to see a therapist. I chose a man, who I knew was gay, but did not appear *fey*. My father did not know that the man was gay. In the second session I told my father about the experience I was having of being surrounded by the constant dying of my friends from AIDS. He said, "Why should I care about them? I don't know them." I looked at the therapist, who said nothing. It obviously did not occur to my father that I or my therapist would find this hurtful. This was an opportunity for the therapist to help my father understand the consequence of his actions, but the man did nothing. I'm sure that if my father had said something sexually inappropriate, the therapist would have intervened. If my father had taken out a crack pipe and started smoking, the therapist would have intervened. I have never been sexually abused and my father was never an addict, but his comments about AIDS were indicative of what he thought was appropriate behavior. The therapist made a judgment call that this kind of homophobia was reasonable enough to not merit intervention. It was a projection of his own oppression experiences and his own lack of self-esteem as a gay man. He may also have wanted my father's approval. Whatever his own issues were, it undermined my opportunity to witness my father hear from someone other than me that his statements were inappropriate.

My father refused to return. He said that instead of these sessions he would meet me for lunch once a week, but no matter how many times I asked him to, he never did. Like most shunners, he knew that a truthful conversation would mean having to take responsibility for his own cruelty, and since no one but me wanted him to, he had no reason to. If he had been court ordered, he would have had to. And I wish that had been an option. I needed a power larger than my father to give him information about his behavior. To make him keep his promises.

Looking back, I have to acknowledge that my father grew up in a household of people who were severely traumatized by war, anti-Semitism, and poverty. His adopted sister, with whom he was raised, was abandoned by her father to be killed by Czarist soldiers, but instead she witnessed her mother and brother being murdered by Cossacks as she hid in a fireplace. My father's mother grew up in a situation so profoundly deprived that her family was on the border of starvation and literally did not have shoes. My father's father came to America alone as a young child. Neither of my father's parents, nor his grandparents, had basic civil rights in their birth countries. They did not have the right to be educated, to own property, or to practice their religion. Clearly my father grew up among the profoundly traumatized, and he needed treatment himself to be able to emotionally reconnect enough to be able love his lesbian daughter. If that therapist had been engaged, prepared, and skilled with the issues of familial homophobia, projection of the traumatized, and positive modes of intervention, all of this could have been broached.

If the therapist had intervened, my father might

have had a better life. He might have had the satisfaction of loving me and being proud of me. After all, I have spent my life doing good things. With intervention, he could have been helped to know this. It would have made him happier.

• In my mid-thirties, I asked my mother to come into counseling with me. The therapist was a referral, and she looked like an obvious lesbian. This gave her no authority with my mother, and she kept trying to establish some. My mother said, "Why should I be overjoyed that Sarah is a homosexual?" The therapist didn't want to contradict her for fear of losing her authority. She therefore allowed these abusive behaviors to become reinscribed, and since there was no one stopping them, the room became a repeat of the kind of cruelty I had already lived with for twenty years.

During the few sessions that took place, my mother said that she and my sister had a secret, but she was not allowed to tell me what it was. My sister forbade her. The therapist said nothing about these manipulations. Entering that room was like entering a humiliation cell. My mother had free reign to repeat any homophobic violation, and the therapist did not know how to intervene to protect me, without giving up her credibility with my mother. Like all gay people, I was just expected to bear it, no matter what its impact. It was not supposed to have any consequence on me because there was some unspoken agreement that I inherently deserved to be treated that way. I later found out from another source that the secret my sister had decided to impose was that she was pregnant. Like my brother excluding me from his wedding, she wisely chose an event that was rooted in heterosexual privilege to exploit the homophobia of my parents.

My mother also came from a background of trauma, oppression, and mass murder. Her father also came here alone from Russia. His sister was exterminated in the Holocaust at Baba Yar. My mother's grandmother was a civilian killed in World War I, and my maternal grandmother's two brothers and two sisters were also murdered in the Holocaust. My mother's father was wanted by the police for desertion but lied to my grandmother and married her under a false name. My grandmother only discovered the truth about her husband when he was arrested. As a consequence of anti-Semitism and war, my mother grew up without an extended family and without grandparents. She had no experience of familial longevity. Her own mother, who had been educated in Austro-Hungary and could read and write five languages, lost all her status when she became a war refugee. My grandmother and grandfather washed other people's clothing for a living. My mother's father died because of inadequate health care, and her mother lived with us all my life because she had no insurance or savings. As a young person, my mother was close to people who were victimized by the blacklist.

I believe that these untreated and unacknowledged traumas made my mother fear difference, fear the disapproval of the dominant culture, which kept her from being able to love her lesbian daughter. I also believe that the destruction of the Jewish people of Europe made both my parents deeply invested in my role as the oldest daughter and my destiny to reproduce the race. However, I also believe that all of this could have been addressed in a proactive, systematic therapy rooted in deep study and interrogation of homophobia, its sources and consequences. If my mother had been supported to see that I am a human being, she could have been proud and happy that I have spent my life working for justice, that I am a hard-working moral and accountable person who has made something interesting and productive out of my life. She could have felt satisfied instead of vicious. But she never could ever have come to this on her own. She NEEDED intervention by other family members, professionals, and authority figures to be able to understand the true meaning of her daughter's life.

I don't excuse my parents, but I loved my father no matter what, and now that he is dead, I still love my mother. I deeply and fundamentally believe in the human responsibility to understand why people do what they do. No matter how cruel what they do actually is. I believe that if someone had intervened, almost anyone, the destructive course of their homophobia could have been reduced or abated.

- Finally, one last try, when my sister excluded my lover and me from knowing my niece, I asked my family to come to meet with my therapist. To this day, I am not allowed to be alone with my niece. As a result, I have not seen her in over ten years, and I also have a nephew and a second niece that I have never seen. My mother tells me that my niece and nephew do not know that I exist. My mother agrees with this exclusion because, as she says, if I were able to be alone with my niece or nephew, I would "tell them that their parents are homophobes." Again it is not the truth that is the problem, but the telling of the truth that justifies punishment. Whether or not they are homophobic, I do not know. But I do know that they ruthlessly exploit homophobia instead of interrupting it. One of my motives for writing this book is so that my nieces and nephew will some day understand what happened in our family and why they do not know me. I hope that when this day comes, I will still be alive and that they will come to see me, so that we can talk.

Anyway, my sister refused to participate in the session. But my father, mother, and brother did come. The therapist asked my mother, "How do you feel knowing that your daughter Sarah will never know your grandchild?"

She said, "Sarah has been terrible since the day she was born. When she was born the obstetrician said, 'That is a bad and uncomfortable child.' "

I interpret this to reflect a shift in my mother's thinking about the cause of homosexuality. At first my parents believed that they made me gay. Under the influence of vulgar 1950s theory, they thought that my homosexuality proved that my father was not a strong father figure and that my mother "loved you too much." Later, they came to believe that homosexuality was a biological deficiency, and so by saying that I was bad since the day I was born, my mother, I believe, was reflecting her new wish that I was biologically homosexual from birth. After they left, the therapist told me, "Don't believe anything they say about you. None of it is true." But why didn't he say that to them? Telling me didn't help me. They needed to hear that someone disapproved of their behavior, someone cared about how I was treated. I needed someone to stand up for me, not tell me what I already knew. His own self-oppression kept him from being able to tell them the truth.

In each of these cases, over a thirty-year period, two things were consistent. No therapist that I encountered was able to intervene directly with the homophobia. They had no mechanism for confronting it and no method for modeling appropriate behavior for my family. All they could do was whisper to me in secret that what my family was doing was wrong. And secondly, and most importantly, my parents never had the opportunity to change their behavior because no one with any currency or authority in their lives, ever confronted them about the morality of what they were doing. Clearly, they were not capable of changing on their own.

What is essentially wrong about the say-nothing-and-separate approach is that it allows the homophobes to own the family. The therapist must begin from the assumption that the gay person is an equal human being and has equal rights and needs to have a family. Therapists have to bring this perspective actively to the process. Through their actions, statements, methods, they must actively embody a reversed value in which it is the homophobe who is destroying the family, not the homosexual. They have to identify ORIGINATING ACTIONS and then show their consequences, not allow pathologizing consequences to be reinterpreted as justifications. To blame the distress and pain of the gay family member for the infliction of that pain is like blaming someone for ruining your furniture when in fact they bled all over it because you shot them.

Ultimately, what is essential is activism *within the psychotherapy industry* for ways to confront the sickness of homophobia in therapeutic terms. Families should be able to be court-ordered into homophobia treatment programs. Schools, businesses—any institution that provides counseling or mediation—should treat the homophobic family members as the cause of the problem. Interventionist methods must be developed to assert, immediately, within one or two sessions, that it is the homophobia that is pathological. Whispering this to victimized gay people while being silent in the face of their persecutors is morally wrong and therapeutically disastrous.

The trauma of familial homophobia on the individual is not understood nor addressed therapeutically. Homophobic trauma is not a recognized category of experience. For the most part, victimized gay people, unless they have been physically assaulted, are expected to grin and bear it. They are expected to be made better and stronger by the cruelty they face instead of being diminished and destabilized. In over twenty-five years of therapy, I have never encountered a therapist who understood the primacy of homophobic trauma on a person's well-being, and I have never seen any systematic approach to treatment. I have never heard an idea about homophobia from a therapist that was new to me. I have never been handed a book that illuminated the experience, nor was I ever referred to or given the name of anyone who was an expert in the field. Basically, I was told repeatedly that these experiences were not central to my condition, which was simply wrong.

The therapist's own sense of self is an essential part of the problem. Heterosexual therapists who harbor fantasies of their own neutrality, who continue to believe that their own sexuality is neutral but that homosexuality needs to have its origins interrogated—these grandiose individuals should be steered into treatment before being unleashed on patients. Obviously, the damage they do to gay clients through their condescending self-position is dramatic. The damage that they do to heterosexual clients is also huge—by communicating their own sense of heterosexuality as neutral, they reinforce their clients in pathologizing the gay people in their lives.

The lack of development of straight and gay therapists on these issues has a chain reaction of destruction. If therapists are going to continue to counsel their clients to separate from their homophobic families and create gay families, then they have a responsibility to support their clients in facing and dealing with problems, negotiating and behaving responsibly to their own partners. If therapists treating gay people encourage cutting-off, withholding, and shunning, then they are making it impossible for the replacement gay family they envision to actually exist. Gay people have not been apologized to; they have not experienced their own families following through, being reliable; they have experienced being treated with a differentiated degree of respect based on their lack of status. It is obvious why they would in turn be unreliable, be unable to apologize, be disrespectful, not keep their promises to the gay people they love. Or be desperate to cling to relationships that are sexually dead, spiritually diminishing or infantilizing. Of course straight people violate each other, and of course there are some gay people who keep their promises. But the gay family will only equal the straight family when gay people are expected by law, tradition, and each other to be as consistent and accountable to each other through transition, crisis, and change as traditional families are expected to be. Right now, this is not an idea that I have ever heard expressed by any therapist. When gay people extend the arm of the cruelty of family, courts, and culture on their lovers, it is a disordered behavior. One to be identified and treated, not justified and reinforced.

Now, one of the problems inherent in this system is that therapists are not supervised; there is no standard of accountability. Straight therapists carry their own history of condescending to or demeaning gay people that they may wish to justify. Gay therapists with gay clients in particular carry their own homophobic trauma and are also subconsciously aware that their clients are devalued people. They are just as vulnerable to the power of suggestion as anyone else. The therapists are essentially free to act out and project their own pathologies and inadequacies on clients, who in turn have no recourse. And they are able to advise clients in behavior toward others without ever hearing what those others think and without ever being accountable for the consequences of that behavior on them.

In the same way that a therapist who has himself been a victim of homophobia may not have the tools to help his patient achieve what he himself was excluded from, dominant culture therapists may easily reinforce the supremacy behavior of their dominant culture clients. A homophobic therapist may encourage a client to keep her child away from the client's homosexual sister even though it is the homophobia (or the sibling manipulation of parental prejudice to raise her own currency within the homophobic family) that has created the problematic relationship in the first place. If the therapist does not understand how familial homophobia works and has never heard from the sister, she may be supporting her client in cruel and sick behavior that will deprive the client's child of a rich, loving relationship with her own aunt. The therapist's own prejudices and ignorance are projected onto the patient's unjustified behavior, sanctifying it with tragic consequences for the child who will never know her aunt.

With feminist therapists and lesbian clients this projection can have even more destructive consequences, because the dynamic is gendered—built around two people who have a deprivation of rights for both gender and sometimes sexuality. Feminist therapy in particular has been a great advocate of cut-offs, withholding, and refusal to communicate, which are the behavior patterns of the unaccountable. They repeatedly construct their lesbian patients as endangered by negotiation, so debilitated by sexual abuse (or metaphoric sexual abuse, "violation") as to be exempt from responsible behavior toward others, and people whose only power is to refuse and withhold.

It is my experience that therapists often encourage lesbian clients toward the "no" position, which they falsely construct as a symbol of power. Heavily influenced by discourses on sexual abuse, incest, and rape, sexual violation has become a predominant paradigm at the core of the therapy of disenfranchised people, just as it is in the larger homophobic culture. Both treat the lesbian as a predator, because she wants to be heard. The model is enforced with any relationship that "threatens" the client. The differentiation between the actual threat of a dangerous sexually abusing parent or assailant is conflated with the "perceived threat" of a friend or lover who may, through depth of feeling or spoken truth, be revealing something that the client needs support to hear. I have never experienced or heard of a lesbian therapist strongly supporting a client to not cut off or shun, but rather to negotiate and face and deal with problems, even if doing so would make them uncomfortable. Yet, repeatedly I have experienced and heard of lesbian therapists encouraging cutoff and shunning, regardless of their client's role in the problematic relationship.

Remember, the therapeutic position as currently constructed is itself a position that rests its power on withholding, cut-off, and unaccountability. The therapist withholds information about herself that may reveal projections onto her patients. Perhaps she has used the courts to deprive her child of access to another female parent. Or if she is straight, perhaps she has manipulated social homophobia to get a better job, or to elevate herself within her own family. The client will never know.

The client may not even know if the gay therapist is in fact gay. Whereas straight people disclose immediately by wearing wedding rings or having pictures on their desks, gay therapists often use more coded methods like having particular books on their shelves. (I've walked into a therapist's office and seen my own books on the shelf even as the therapist never disclosed her homosexuality.) And most importantly, they advise, instruct, and reinforce behavior in their clients that can destroy the lives of others who will never be able to make them accountable. If the client feels that the therapist is dishonest, on a power trip, cheating them financially, lying about credentials, improperly terminating, whatever, it is almost impossible to successfully petition an intervening body. No wonder so much therapeutic advice replicates the protective shield of institutionalized non-accountability that therapists create for themselves.

Whether the therapist is reinforcing the straight client's homophobic cruelty, or reinforcing the gay clients' extension of familial, social, legal, and cultural homophobic cruelty, the therapist is never accountable for the consequences of his actions on the third party, even though the therapist may be the only authority figure, or *in loco parentis* figure, in the lives of the client or her victim. Since homophobic parents instruct their straight children in homophobia, the straight therapist is the key authority figure who can reparent the homophobe away from replicating the parents' cruelty against gay family members. Because homophobic parents cannot impart helpful life advice to their gay children, and withholding results in lack of communication and lack of information, the unaccountable therapist projecting onto her own client becomes overly determining in reinforcing negative behavior.

Because so many of us do not have healthy supportive families of origin, the therapist treating lesbian patients may be the only parental figure who listens and accepts the client's homosexuality. Within the absence of family, cultural representation and legal protection, therapists have an inordinate amount of influence and power to determine the actions of their clients. Because of homophobia, many couples are not acknowledged by parental figures for the good they bring into each other's lives. Most lesbian couples only receive affirmation internally, within the relationship. Once the external forces overwhelm the internal ones, a counter-homophobia therapeutic emphasis must be focused on delineating, with clarity and precision, what gifts the women bring to each other, what specific reciprocities they have shown, what actions they have taken to acknowledge and help each other. This may be the only time in the life of the relationship that the value of the other human being is affirmed publicly and one partner's responsibility to the other is insisted upon. Since this occurs nowhere else in our daily life, the therapist is the one person who has the opportunity to model and insist on keeping promises, negotiating, treating other despised gay people with respect and responsibility. But to do this, they have to supersede their own oppression experiences and overcome the lack of articulated clarity about the functions of familial homophobia and its consequences, as well as the lack of specificity about how to treat both homophobic behavior and homophobic trauma.

DOING TO LOVERS AS OTHERS HAVE DONE TO US/HER

One of the most obvious expressions of gay-on-gay shunning, as an extension of family and governmental oppression, is the use of the court system by one gay parent to deny custody to the other. In the late 1990s, there were about a dozen cases like this around the country. The number has grown exponentially since then. Sadly, a number of these plaintiffs claimed sole custody on the grounds that the relationship, by virtue of not being legal, was illegitimate, and that, therefore, they had no responsibility to be accountable to their partner's relationship to their children. This is the most stark, while emblematic, example of how gay people extend the hand of anti-gay oppression against each other.

I interviewed Kate Kendell, director of the San Francisco–based National Coalition for Lesbian Rights (NCLR), about the budding trend of gay people using the courts to deny their partner's access to children that the two had raised together. Although this conversation took place in the 1990s, the questions of morality, responsibility, and group dynamics in lesbian and gay communities are still the same. In the 1990s the relationship of gays and lesbians to the legal system was in a state of insane contradiction. Sodomy was still illegal. Basic civil rights varied from city to city and state to state, as they do today. Gay marriage was still illegal in all fifty states. Today it is illegal in forty-five. A number of cities and states were holding public referenda on repealing already existing gay-rights bills, or creating pre-emptive anti-gay legislation ensuring that no gay rights bills could ever be passed in that area, as they are still doing today. In 2008, Kendell was part of the leadership in California to defeat Proposition 8, an anti-gay ballot measure designed to reverse a legislative decision legalizing gay marriage. Even though Obama won California in the election, Prop 8 was passed and the 36,000 people who had experienced gay marriage had their marriages called into question.

In our discussion, we focused on the psychology of lesbians going to court either to try to keep shared custody of a child they had raised in a now destroyed relationship, or to prohibit the former lover from having access to a child she had raised. It was bizarre and yet predictable to watch lesbians use the state that dehumanized them as a tool to diminish each other. After all, all homosexual lovers have watched the person who has given them pleasure, friendship, caring, love, and kindness be repeatedly humiliated by their family, by cultural representation, and/or by the state. So, when the time came when it was convenient to pretend away any responsibility to that person, the simplest thing to do was to imitate the cruelty they had already always endured. The question was, when a lesbian decides to treat her lover as badly as the lover's family, culture, and the state had always treated her, would the courts be willing to enforce that repetition? And if so, whose responsibility is it to interfere on the gay person's behalf with the ferocity that the state interferes against them?

· · ·

Kate Kendell is a very busy woman. She has an adult daughter back in Utah, a girlfriend/wife, and a young son in San Francisco. She is an attorney with a job that requires a lot of traveling and late hours. But a lot of her time these days is spent trying to understand the lesbian mind.

As executive director of the National Center for Lesbian Rights (NCLR), Kate is on the forefront of recent court battles of a very disturbing nature. It is not the religious right, not homophobic parents, and not disgruntled ex-husbands who are trying to deny basic parenting rights to lesbians. No, recently there have been more and more court cases involving lesbians who raised children in the context of a relationship, and once the relationship ended, the biological mothers are going to court to keep their old girlfriends away from the children. On what grounds? These women are claiming that they never were a "family" as the courts understand that word, and that their ex-girlfriends are not eligible for the rights and responsibilities that a real family involves. So, they claim, after all those years of political agitation, the dominant culture was right. Lesbian love is not real love and results in no responsibility from one partner to the other. Tough stuff.

The same women now who are using the state to keep children from their ex-girlfriends previously would have had their kids taken away if they had been originally coupled with men and then came out. Now they are "the man" because they have the state on their side. I asked Kendell if people are so corruptible that as soon as they have the power of the state they start bullying and if the previous experience of being marginalized has any impact.

"That's a very cynical but I think sadly pretty accurate assessment," she said. "Any other explanation is even more cynical. If it's not that these biological parents simply are using power just because they've got it, then it has to do with something about the lesbian bio-parent psyche which could be about ownership, a sense of a child as property."

"Does it have to do with their sense of their own femininity, or being *a real woman* because they have a child?"

"Clearly," she said, "we all have this sense, and probably all have an experience growing up where we got the message that if you are a mother and you got divorced, you should have custody, you should seek custody, you should want it and if you didn't there's something wrong with you. But what these bio-parents are doing is so beyond that, because in most of these cases, no one is saying that the biological parent doesn't get custody. She will. She does. It is generally conceded by the other parent. All the non-bio parent wants is to fill the shoes of what is a very common and easily recognizable model, the true non-custodial father model. She's the non-custodial parent. She'll have visitation every other weekend and on Wednesday evenings. That's the standard rule. And will have some role in the child's life. This is a model that we've seen billions of times in every heterosexual divorce in which children were involved. It's not as if we're saying to biological mothers, 'You need to accept an entirely different model because you're a lesbian family' or that she needs to give up something more than a heterosexual woman would have to give up. No, what we're saying is that we should play by the same rules. These biological mothers are saying 'No, we don't have to play by the same rules because the legal system doesn't recognize what I have as a family. So, I'm not going to recognize it as a family either because it is no longer convenient for me to do so.' "

"For the women who do this," Kendell continued, "it is classic victim psychology that puts them in a position of fighting for the illegitimate. Maybe it's because of past victimization or internalized homophobia or a sense of themselves as really out of the protection of the larger society. It's why lesbian and gay people are horribly racist. It's a sense of completely not getting it and not understanding the ultimate harm."

I suggested to Kendell that the only times in their lives they've ever had any state power is when they became mothers. All their lives they were treated as lesbians; suddenly they're being treated as straight women—and having the power associated with heterosexuality. But the person on the other side is not a man.

"No, she's a lesbian and she is really now the outsider," Kendell illuminated. "It is a sense of being able to victimize the victim."

Kendell has talked to several people that she has opposed in court. "What they say is, 'Well, she never really was a parent. She never wanted to be a parent. I never considered her to be a parent.' It's all justifications for why she's taking the positions she's taking."

"Do they believe that or do they know that they are lying about the past?"

"Whether they wake up at three o'clock in the morning and feel sick to their stomach because they know they are perpetuating a huge charade, I don't know." Kendell replied. "Now, what's also interesting is that we have never ever seen or heard of a similar case involving gay men."

Kate and I were talking about lesbians, people who are a-socialized. What we were seeing was the lives of people who are in many ways pushed outside of the norms of the society, and as a result can act in a way where they don't care about the consequence, don't care about how they are viewed because they don't feel any stake in social agreement about being accountable to each other or a loyalty to social order, even within a lesbian community.

"I used to say that these cases broke my heart because I expected and wanted so much more from women in my community. If someone would have said to me, before I knew about this phenomenon, that this was happening, and it is probably going to happen a lot more, I would not have believed them. Especially that you can convince yourself that taking a parent away from your child doesn't do damage to that child? When all else fails, that is the thing that I'm most baffled by. How can you say that a seven-year-old, who calls this person "Momma" and has seen her every single day of her life, should be told one day that she's never going to see Momma again?"

Why is this happening? Why are so many lesbians willing to act so crazily and destructively?

"It comes," she said, "from a place that is so victimized that you don't even understand when you've moved from being the victim to the oppressor. I'm convinced that the reason most of these cases proceed is that by and large, most women who take this terrible position do have a cadre of friends supporting them. Most of them are not completely alone. They usually have a cadre of close friends who say, 'Oh yeah, she was a bitch. I never liked her.' Not appreciating that there is a child in the center of this family. Generally the biological parents who take this position have at least a handful of other lesbians who support her in her actions. The community needs to be able to put sufficient pressure on the bio-mom's friends to tell her, 'We can't support you in this strategy.' "

This is what makes Kendell so interesting. She has articulated a community-based approach to the problem. Since the relationship between lesbians and the court system and lesbians and the state is an ever changing relationship, creating a stigma within the community is the way to regulate people's behavior. To make amoral lesbians realize that actually someone does care about how they act and that there is someone who notices and cares enough that the woman in question has to be accountable. To tell her that she does live within a moral system. It's about the responsibilities of not being alone. It's kind of brilliant.

"I'll use whatever I have to," Kendell says. "I think these cases are so ultimately destructive and given the failure of the legal system to catch up, I and other advocates will use whatever we have to try to protect our families, our family law, and these kids. We must stop bio-moms from taking this position."

Interestingly, Kendell is taking a group of people, lesbians, who nobody cares about. People who, when something bad happens to them, have no one to protect them and, when they are doing something wrong, have no one to intervene and tell them that they shouldn't. People who have lived in an emotionally anarchistic state. So, basically, I can do anything nasty to you and no one is going to tell me that it's not okay and no one is going to help you. We have relationships which are illusions of safety. But we don't have family support and we don't have societal support. We're floating, emotional satellites. What Kendell is trying to do is to anchor this behavior by creating a community responsibility so that if someone is acting immorally, a friend will intervene. I asked Kendell, "Do you think that that can be used on other terms besides children?"

She replied, "It can be used for good or for ill. It is a strategy that is very risky. Because you live in Utah and you're a member of ACT UP and you chain yourself to Temple Square trying to give light to the anti-gay activities of the Latter Day Saints Church, and your friends are saying, 'Stop it, you're causing too much trouble and making it hard for us.' That is an unfortunate use of community pressure. It is a tactic that today I am an agent in creating."

"If your family was homophobic," I asked her. "If your birth family said to you, 'You can't be near your niece or we're not going to recognize your achievements or we're not going to be accountable or value your life,' would it—based on your concept of the community—be my responsibility to go to your family of origin and tell them that their behavior is not acceptable because I am in a community that is accountable to you? If I'm going to condemn you when you're horrible, I also have to defend you when someone else is treating you unfairly, right?"

"It gives some substance to the word 'community' to think that there would be such an ethic and sense of responsibility," she replied. "Whenever I talk about the 'queer community,' I think of the quotation marks in my head. I don't know that there really is a queer community—the word connotes a collective responsibility, collective caretaking, collective concern for the welfare of those who are members. I think we've got a community in only the loosest sense. But virtually every member of the queer community has their own little community of friends that can have influence."

"Kate, have you ever gone to the birth families of any of your friends and told them that their homophobia toward your friend was inappropriate?"

Kendell said no. I asked her if she would be willing to do so.

"Yeah. Part of what the issue is for taking on a sense of community responsibility is that you have to have nothing to lose yourself. Even our suggesting that there should be community pressure on these biological moms to not take this position—well, the only way that's going to happen is if people have nothing to lose, or see it in their self-interest."

But they have something to lose. And standing up for somebody else is uncomfortable. People will allow almost anything to occur rather than be uncomfortable.

"True," Kendell replied, "we don't behave that way, but we could. We at NCLR feel that this particular situation is one where setting up a sense that there should be a community standard opposed to bio-moms doing this is in the best interest of the broader community."

Yes, because there are children involved. But I asked Kendell, "What if there were just adults involved?"

"They still should treat each other honorably and abide by their promises to each other."

Here, I expressed my larger concern. If you've been told your whole life that you are worthless, what good is your word? When I have done political organizing in a lesbian context, one of the things that I learned there was that we had a constituency of people, many of whom had been told all their lives that they were nothing. Many had never had or used power, did not know how to be proactive, felt that their only power was to be obstructive. A lot of times lesbians would come into a room determined that the only way they could express themselves was to stop something. When we created the Lesbian Avengers in 1992, we had to create a rule that if you disagreed with a proposal you couldn't just critique it; you had to make a better suggestion. This drove people wild because they didn't have the skill or authority to be proactive and create things, to negotiate, to face and deal with problems, to propose solutions. They only knew how to obstruct and destroy. That's what you're dealing with here. We have it on a lot of different fronts. If we take your idea and expand it—what you are talking about is a real gay family.

If you are in a functional straight family and your husband is treating you like shit, your brother might drive over to the house and tell him that that's not okay. But if it's your girlfriend, nobody cares. Your family is not going to do anything, and your "friends" are going to stay out of it. You're alone. If we want to have a gay family that is equal to the straight family, we need to have an ethic of intervention and accountability that functions along the lines of their official ethic at its most functional. What you are doing is the beginning of something that can really transform what our lives are like.

"To be fair," Kendell responded, "it's what advocates in the domestic violence community have been talking about as well. The invisibility of queer-on-queer domestic violence and the collusion of the friends who know what's happening and then ignore it is tantamount to approving of it and allowing it to go forward."

"What is the difference between intervening in the life of your friends and bringing in the state? Especially when the state won't support gay people? Should we be more like the mafia and take care of things internally?"

"You've got somebody who's not going to allow visitation, you go over there, you sit down and you tell them this isn't okay. The reason that tactic can work and the reason I suggest it is because I know it happens and I've seen women insulated by their friends. I know if they lose the last bit of cover they've got, those few close friends who are all they've got left, supporting them in an immoral action, it is a very rare person who will say, 'Fuck you all, I'll fly by myself.' It is a rare person who won't succumb to some degree to close friends saying, 'You can't do this,' because it is all we have."

Basically, what I took from the conversation is that if someday a woman tries to keep her kid away from its other parent, the community can intervene; if someone's family is abusively homophobic to them, the community can intervene; if your lover is abusive and destroying the fabric of your life, the community can intervene—in other words, we can have a social structure.

"The legal system does not simply require that we play by the same rules as heterosexual couples," Kendell said. "Eventually, the system will do that, but until they catch up, I can't demand that bio-moms always be rational, because they're not going to. The only thing we've got left is to say that friends will intervene and say, 'You can't do this. We're not going to support this.' It is in the long-term best interest of the child, the couple, and the community. If the community could really take responsibility about us being honorable to each other, then it doesn't matter what the legal system does; then we don't have to pay tens of thousands of dollars to attorneys; there's actually more certainty and less wrenching if there is a sense of responsibility. We are responsible for the decisions we make with each other."

THIRD PARTY INTERVENTION

The Human Obligation

What I find most moving about Kate's analysis is the way she frames the cruelty of the lesbian partner against her lover as an act of projection. A lesbian who has had no rights and who has been traumatized by the system all her life suddenly has the euphoric emotional catharsis of being able, finally, to stick it to someone else. This reversal is so intoxicating that many will fight like dogs for that ecstatic feeling of domination. It's an especially potent power when it is held over someone who knows their sexual truth, the very truths for which they have themselves been victimized. The fact that the originating cruelty was from other people whose privileges keep them out of reach seems not to matter. The glee of doing it to someone else, who has even less protection, prevails.

After all, some cruelty comes from privilege and some comes from trauma. Their motivations and solutions are entirely different. But their impact on the victim is the same.

When privileged people scapegoat, they do it from repetition, arrogance, habit. The pleasure is the pleasure of entitlement, the inflated sense of one's self as neutral, natural, and right. But when a perpetrator scapegoats from a place of trauma, it is almost always an act of projection. It was her father who sexually abused her, but it's the lover who can truly reach her sexually who suddenly becomes Satan. It is her drunken parents who never could face and deal with a problem, but it is her lover making her open the credit card bills, whom she can in turn humiliate and cathartically dehumanize. And because the lover is herself unprotected, the lesbian can impulsively act out her pain on her partner without fear of consequence.

Kendell identifies this as a kind of re-victimization, where one devalued person "does not keep her promises" to another devalued person and does this "not understanding the ultimate harm" of her actions. She says, "It comes from a place that is so victimized that you don't even understand when you've moved from being the victim to being the oppressor." And she identifies the foundation of this cruel behavior as "a cadre of friends" who support the woman in her illegitimate action.

Being on the receiving end of intense homophobia from family, which is supposed to be the central support structure in a person's life, is a severely traumatizing experience, which creates a resulting vulnerability that in turn makes the victim again susceptible to these kinds of projections from other oppressed people. Remember, people scapegoat the powerless because there is no consequence for doing so. If there was a consequence, they would stop. Having no family support because you are gay, being pathologized for being gay and then being blamed for the consequences of that pathologization, these *twists* create a target for the projection of others. These experiences make one extremely vulnerable to being blamed because the blamers know, instinctively, that no one will stand up and disrupt the process. Observing someone else's vulnerability is suggestive. It embeds the message that this person can be violated without consequence. It is the corrosive power of suggestion.

Actually, knowledge about other people should *increase* your responsibility toward them. If you know that someone has emphysema, you are required by moral code to not exhale cigarette smoke at that person. If you know someone is an alcoholic, you don't spike that person's drink. If you know that someone has no family, you don't invite them into yours and then shut them out of it again. If you know that someone cannot walk, you don't hide their crutches. If you know that someone has been scapegoated, you don't scapegoat them. If you know that someone has been excluded from the children in his or her family, you don't promise the person a relationship with yours and then withhold it. And if you do, you don't blame them for being devastated. If you know that someone is thirsty, you don't pour the water into the sand. If you know that someone is being shunned, you don't shun the person. If you know that someone has no place to go for Thanksgiving or Passover, you invite them. And if you tell them they are always welcome, don't be surprised when they show up at your door. These principles should be obvious. Yet, bullies abound. There are a lot of people looking for the catharsis of scapegoating and cruelty to give themselves a pleasurable feeling. And there are a lot of people who will defend their right to do anything that creates impulsive pleasure no matter how much pain it causes others.

When someone is being shunned because they have no institution of support, whether by a family, the state, the arts and entertainment—industrial complex, society, or a projecting similarly oppressed person, there is one case in which third-party intervention is the moral imperative: when they ask you to. Even if the perpetrator tries to obstruct. Refusing people who are begging for protective intervention re-wounds them. It leaves them worse off than they were before.

Intervening on behalf of a person who is being scapegoated is the positive choice on a number of fronts:

1. It creates integrity and dignity for the intervener, even if the intervention is not successful.
2. It shows the person being victimized that some-

one cares about how they are treated and supports them even if the intervention is not successful.

3. It gives perpetrators the knowledge that their behavior is morally offensive. Rewarding them with silence withholds this information from them. Forcing perpetrators to justify their actions, engaging them in interactive conversation about why they are doing what they are doing may help to articulate other ways of behaving that perpetrators cannot come up with themselves.

4. It creates consequences for the perpetrators. The more people who protest their cruelty, the less likely they are to maintain it. Only truly pathological people will continue to shun another regardless of how much it costs them.

5. It creates a zeitgeist of response that can protect other people from having to suffer in the same way in the future.

Yet, despite this, one of the big obstacles to third-party intervention that could end this suffering is the perpetrators' frequent claim that their behavior is "private." They experience their shunning and projection onto gay people as somehow their inherent "right." This active, assaultive abandonment gets falsely constructed as the perpetrator's "privacy" somehow outside of the realm of accountability. As though it were a benign individual choice like wanting your eggs over easy or scrambled. Because it is instead an extension of a huge structural system of injustice, its enforcement by individuals is not only their business. They make a kind of individual version of states' rights arguments, where states want the right to legally discriminate on the basis of race, gender, or sexuality. Individuals have a dialogic relationship with the state, in that they mimic each other's methods. They may claim that it is their "right" to exclude a gay family member, or to exploit a lover's lack of power. But, actually, it's not their right. No one has a "right" to destroy someone else's life, but only third parties can stop them. This power to exploit someone else's lack of rights is so dear to the perpetrators that they think it is their private property, out of the realm of other people's reach. And they theorize other people's wish to end the cruelty as itself violating.

I am so impressed and intrigued by this construction. That to shun and scapegoat with assaultive and dehumanizing actions are rights and private while to intervene to stop this cruelty is somehow itself the violation.

Of course, we've seen this twisted construction many times in history. Segregationists positioned themselves as a culture being trampled, violated, and invaded by federal laws forcing integration and its implied miscegenation. Suffragists looking for full responsibility and participation were depicted as libertines—irresponsible and socially parasitic, violating the "moral" family fiber with a kind of sexual threat. Supporters of abortion rights are depicted as child murderers. Gay rights means that homosexuals will have sex with your children and should be kept away from their own children, or must have children to matter. Over and over the person actively seeking equality, accountability, and full communication between equal parties is constructed as some kind of violator, destroying "privacy" rights, and often with an implied sexual threat. It's as though the *information* that the other person has feelings, ideas, is equally fully human, would violate the chastity, the unknowing state of the shunner's life if the victim was allowed to participate and negotiate, speak. This information is positioned as inherently sexually threatening. And the shunner is self-righteously passionate about defending their purity, their right to exclude.

Atina Grossman's fascinating, complex book *Jews, Germans, and Allies: Close Encounters in Occupied Germany* (Princeton University Press) gives a crystal-clear example of perpetrators re-inventing themselves as victims. She confronts and analyzes in depth how quickly German civilians began complaining to U.S. occupying forces about their suffering and mistreatment at the hands of the Nazis that they themselves had democratically elected. Grossman documents how quickly the United States and Russia capitulated to this idea, the United States abandoning any real effort at de-Nazification almost immediately. In the German Democratic

Republic (East Germany), Stalin quickly absolved Germans of any real responsibility so that he could win their easy loyalty. As Stalin said, "The Hitlers come and go. The German Volk remains." This strategy of laying no responsibility created a class of victims who never experienced justice. They never experienced public acknowledgments of cruelty, fascism, and injustice. In my own experience, the lingering lack of accountability by perpetrators severely harms victims in the long term. It alienates them from themselves and their core values.

When the family is excluding and persecuting a gay person who is asking for intervention, people who know and come into contact with that family have a moral imperative to tell them that what they are doing is wrong. Especially other straight people, work colleagues, neighbors. Perpetrators scapegoat the gay person because they believe that no one cares. They interpret the silence of others as a reward of approval. Only if they are made to feel a negative consequence for their actions will their actions change. It is the responsibility of others to create that consequence.

The shunning of the gay person within a family is morally wrong. Whether it is expressed through actual exclusion, diminishment, or pathologization, the process of humiliating someone who has not done anything wrong is never justified. Families have responsibilities to their members, the responsibility of longevity. When a person is not driven out by cruelty or kept from family events or from children, that person has the opportunity to re-experience family members over and over again at events and—if they are not excluded—through different group decision-making experiences. If they are given information about family crises and achievements, joys and pains, and if their crises and achievements, joys and pains are acknowledged as those of someone equally human, then processes occur by which different problems are eclipsed and different tendernesses are won. When people are excluded from these processes, the relationship cannot transform precisely because of the refusal of interactive problem solving, i.e., shunning.

In an appropriate family structure, different members are called on at different moments because of their different skills. In a shunning family, the gay person's true skills and abilities are pretended away so that the heterosexual family members can create the delusion of supremacy and importance for themselves. If gay family members are included, they are sometimes expected to make family needs primary because their lives are not perceived as important. They may not be consulted in a way that allows them to fully contribute but instead are simply told what to do. Whether through over-expectation or shunning, the gay person is often not allowed to be fully human.

When gay people have the rare experience of being fully humanized within their family, they often choose to prioritize that family over friends or other relationships that may not themselves have familial support. Having a family is not considered to be the privilege that it is; instead it is theorized as neutral. So other people's lack is theorized as their fault in the way that poverty and illness are also theorized as the fault of the poor and the ill. This way of thinking enables people with a humanizing family to falsely see it as a natural outgrowth of their own goodness and deserving nature. Sometimes members of good families rely so completely on the ever-present support structure of their family that they don't bother to face and deal with problems with friends, because they know that no matter how they treat others, they will have unconditional familial support. The loving family keeps them from taking responsibility for how they treat others. A truly humanizing family will demand that their gay family member treat their lovers honorably. A special risk for a moderately accepting family is that they may not view their gay family member's relationships as requiring moral responsibility and may resent their partners.

In this way, the "cadre" of friends that Kate Kendell described as the foundation of immoral behavior can in fact be the gay person's family, holding no expectation standard for how they treat another homosexual. In a healthy, non-homophobic family, a gay family member's closest friends and lovers also have support from that family, are treated like family, can go to the family for intervention and protection.

If the gay family member abandons or projects onto a lover, the family must intervene and support that person by confronting their family member with her capacity and duty to be responsible and accountable. Loving gay family members means believing that they can treat other gay people with full personhood.

When a gay person does not have a healthy family, and a lover extends the cruelty of the family, society, and culture through shunning or abandonment, it is the moral imperative of the people who know them to intervene and advocate for negotiation, acknowledgment, and responsibility.

Unfortunately, this rarely occurs. First, there is a psychology of powerlessness. The gay friends do not see themselves as fully responsible citizens. They do not see their shunned friend as someone deserving of due process. Often the friends privilege the withholder in deference to the fantasy that there is a "private sphere." This is based on the fantasy of a heterosexual family in which that scapegoated person's pain will be heard and tended to by "someone"—a sphere that is someone else's responsibility. But for many gay people, if the gay friends do not intervene, there is no private sphere and that "someone" does not exist.

In fact, people evoke the word "privacy" as justification for refusing to negotiate. They don't have to negotiate; it's their right to privacy. The "private" family doesn't have to account for their treatment of gay people; the "private" citizen doesn't have to account for her treatment of gay people—even those who have shared love with her. Industries like book publishing, theater, film and television production, religion, and education are all private endeavors that have no public accountability to gay people. Even the Saint Patrick's Day parade is legally a private event and is permitted to shun Irish gays and lesbians annually.

The word "privacy" is a justification for maintaining the scapegoating of people who have no private sphere. It's like Carla Harryman's observation that homeless people are not allowed to live in public space because their socially engineered condition is pretended away as their "private" problem. The only right to "privacy" I believe in is when Mastercard wants your social security number. No one has the "private" right to scapegoat another human being no matter how badly they want to. Refusing to treat someone the way that they deserve to be treated by you is not a right. That is a misuse of that concept. In fact, I would argue the opposite. Interactive resolution and communication is a social responsibility. To refuse it is anti-social. People who live in a shared community of colleagues and friends have an overriding social responsibility to promote communication and resolution. And bystanders have the moral responsibility to do everything they can to encourage communication and to discourage shunning.

This distorted thinking comes, of course, from many different streams. One contributor among many is protectionism, and how it has been historically applied to people without rights.

The so-called Progressive Era–discourse of protectionism has been revitalized in many guises. This is the idea that certain experiences and certain knowledge are inherently dangerous for some people, usually those infantilized by lack of rights. In the industrial age, the debate was about women in the workplace. Protectionists once argued that it was in women's best interest to be excluded from the experiences of dangerous or alienating labor. Their opponents argued for women's free agency in the paid labor force as an essential part of economic and psychological autonomy. Some felt that the institution of paid labor was an unfit context for women and chose to preemptively ensure that no woman would have the information (be it enlightening or diminishing) of that experience. Others felt that women and work would dialectically act on and transform each other.

The reproductive rights movement of the 1960s, '70s, and '80s engaged a similar discourse, but its counter-points were religious right-wing organizations. Feminists argued that choices and full information about abortion, birth control, and sexuality improved women's lives. Antifeminists argued that restricting the experience of what they saw to be destructive or immoral choices and information were in women's best interest. If abortion or lesbianism are inherently wrong, keeping women from having this information or these experiences was in their best interest, they said.

In the 1980s this debate resurfaced as internal to feminism. It was recast from the arena of women in the industrial workplace and refocused on the role of women as workers and consumers in the realm of sexual commodification. Some argued that pre-emptive restrictions on women's participation in the production of and access to sexually explicit materials were in women's best interests. Others argued that full availability of information and choices served women's interests. This is a long-standing tension about the pre-emptive restriction of information and experience. In these highly politicized public realms—labor, abortion, pornography—the motives for restricting information seem fairly clear.

At the root of this obstruction is the powerful fact that information allows people to create choices, explore consequences, and act with awareness. But also that knowledge creates responsibilities. Lack of information allows impulsive acting out, without full articulation of possible hopes or outcomes. People who want to pretend that they do not have responsibility to others try to refuse the information that would make them conscious of this responsibility. Active engagement changes the perpetrators (i.e., mitigates or stops or creates consequences for their cruelty). Doing nothing changes the victims (abandons them to being abused). "But you can't change other people!" you may cry. Not so! Ask anyone whose life has been destroyed by someone else's cruelty. Victims are changed. It's perpetrators whom we are told, we cannot transform. As my college professor Audre Lorde used to say, "That you can't change City Hall is a rumor being spread by City Hall."

I would argue that this discourse about the pros and cons of protectionism is just as relevant in the emotional realm. Access to ideas, opinions, and feelings of others allows an individual to create choices, which may lead to change. Restricting the intake of information makes change harder to articulate or imagine. If you will not let someone tell you how your actions are affecting them, then you have no responsibility to acknowledge or rethink your actions. People who are isolated tend to have less information about how others live. They don't hear how other people face and deal with problems, and so they have less information about how to move forward constructively in their own lives, and consequently are more likely to cause harm to others. They hear fewer bad ideas and fewer good ones. Because change is not inherently good, but can be good, not hearing other people's ideas, opinions, and feelings can make it easier to resist negative change. But, by preemptively restricting one's exposure to other people's ideas, experiences, and feelings, one ensures that both negative and positive change will be harder to come by.

Many frightened people organize their lives around the refusal of information: withholding from and avoiding interactivity, screening and not returning phone calls, refusing to have conversations, hiding behind e-mail. They can be privileged people who are frightened by the thought of threats to their privilege. They can be traumatized people who are frightened by accepting the power of their actions. The debate is still one of protectionism, although it is now cast as part of the so-called "private sphere." Hearing about the consequences of your actions on others is falsely described as a violation. People who hide, insist that they have a "right" not to know how their actions affect other people. Their fear of information is so intense that they can describe this information as some kind of violation. They may even use the language of sexual assault to describe how badly they feel when they hear about the consequences of their actions on others. Censors may call authentic gay representation "pornography" or rate it NC-17, as though it is dangerous. Individuals may say that they feel "unsafe" or "assaulted" if someone without rights wants to tell them how their actions make them feel.

Within the family, the legal system, and the arts and entertainment–industrial complex, homosexuals and our accurate expressions are seen as inherently sexually predatory. It is implied and no longer needs to be explained that this is why we should not be included in certain human experiences and representations. Within this construction, the desire to be fully humanized, given due process, be heard, is experienced as sexually violating—the imposition of sex. Only human beings have responsibilities and feelings; vampires and other predatory shadows simply don't have the right. And shunned, victimized, scapegoated homosexuals excluded from their families and from cultural representation do not deserve to be heard. Even by each other.

The sexualized hysteria within familial homophobia and its consequence on lesbian/gay culture itself and representational constrictions converge with this misuse of the feminist "NO." The origin within feminism of the idea of refusal as a "right" comes from early discourse about sex. Women were expected to comply with male demands for sex. We were not considered to possess the right to refuse. By insisting on a woman's right to say "no," feminists transformed paradigms about rape, motherhood, birth control, sexual harassment, and sexual abuse. "No" became a statement that implied a kind of resistance to an inappropriate form of sexual action, There were slogans like "What part of NO don't you understand?" and other political strategies emphasizing refusal as a right.

For reasons that I do not understand, oppression discourse has often been twisted by sexual hysteria into advocating for obstruction over resolution, which is ultimately not in women's best interests. Over time, and in different ways, linking a position to sexual abuse has made that position's righteousness ironclad. Right and wrong have at different times in feminist discourse been defined by perception of sexual threat, whether or not it is accurate. Refusal has become the symbol of self. Self-esteem becomes falsely defined by the right to say "no." The refusal to negotiate, or to treat the other disenfranchised person as a full human being, has taken on a meaning, rooted in fear of sexual violation, that now surpasses sexual violation. Describing a gay family member as a sexual threat to a child, or a pathologized lover as a "stalker," saying that the withholder "feels raped," or that gay people trying to march in the Saint Patrick's Day parade are "violating" the other marchers, and other inflammatory words implying sexual threat are used as metaphors to justify exclusion and refusal to negotiate. As though simply using that vocabulary justifies any action.

Should "no" mean no? Just because someone says "no," does that mean that they are truthful, appropriate, justified? That they should be listened to? And is refusing to obey them really a sexual violation? When a family just does not want their gay relative among them, the industry just does not want the gay character, the landlord just does not want the gay tenant, the lover just does not want her dearest to know their child, does that make it okay? If the victim is powerless, apparently it does. Only when you can force, through third-party intervention, the right to personhood (that is, to due process, to be heard), does that arbitrary, convenient "no" become overridden. Just because someone says "no" doesn't mean that we have to listen.

Silence, refusal, cut-off, and withholding in the dialogic power relation of family, state, love, and cultural representation are not neutral actions. They are aggressive, hostile, abusive actions. They create an on-going infliction of pain that is often not deserved. Whether the shunning comes from privilege or from trauma, the consequence on the victim is profound and deserves intervention.

Frankly, if someone can get a court order to avoid resolution, I think they should be able to get a court order compelling resolution. Telling the truth and being heard, truly understanding one's responsibilities toward others and the consequences of one's actions on another person, is in the best interest of the whole. Even if it is uncomfortable. Some no's are appropriate and would stand up to third-party scrutiny, and some are not. "No, you can't talk to me because you stole my money to buy drugs" is very different from "No, you cannot speak to me because you tell me something about myself that I don't want to hear." The former would be easily explained and the latter withheld and obstructed behind all kinds of victimizing smoke screens.

People love the people they are good to and hate the

people they are cruel to. The object's actual behavior is too often not a factor. No one fears you more than someone who has abused you. As my grandmother, Dora Leibling Yevish, used to say, "The Germans will never forgive the Jews for the Holocaust." In other words, when one person hurts you, they hate you more because you know what they are really like.

The recipient of inappropriate behavior is a witness, has justifiable consequential anger, wants change, and is therefore not trustworthy in the eye of the perpetrator, which is why governments give permits to homophobic Irish people on Saint Patrick's Day and take the gay Irish people trying to participate in the march off to jail. The state trusts the homophobes whom they have long rewarded, and the state mistrusts the gay people whom they have long abused. It has nothing to do with the inherent truth about the gay people or the homophobes and how each group objectively deserves to be treated. It is the Ancient Order of Hibernians who have acted badly, who then withhold, refuse to resolve, thereby avoiding responsibility and accountability. And the oppressed, shunned gay people, whose attempts to get into the parade are treated like sexual violators, are physically restrained, put in handcuffs, and taken away into jail cells. Just because the Hibernians don't want us in and don't want to talk about it doesn't mean that we have to do what they say.

People who have acted fairly have nothing to hide and therefore don't. Despite the twisted sexual morality associated with "no," the withholder, through the active assault of shunning, is often actually the violator. The Ancient Order of Hibernians excludes the gay people claiming that they are dangerous invaders and violators, posing a sexual threat, but actually it is the Hibernians, through their shunning, who are the ones causing harm.

•

WITHHOLDING CREATES TENSION, ACKNOWLEDGMENT CREATES RELIEF

(And This Is Why We Are Talking About Gay Marriage)

We agree that all human beings should have the same legal rights, but here is my question, what does gay marriage really mean? Why do people want it so badly? Is it really all about love, taxes, and extending the special privileges that people receive for being in couples to gay couples as well?

The propaganda campaigns for gay marriage usually feature a perfect couple. They've been together forever, have good solid incomes, one or more happy children. They are perfect, and their perfect union deserves to be protected from the state. The examples are offered over and over of ways this perfect love is vulnerable to the state. If one is sick, the state can keep the other from visitation. If one dies, the state can seize the other's belongings. Bad state.

Re-affirming, as I said above, that everyone should have the same legal rights, I believe marriage has never really been about protecting the relationship from the state. The purpose of marriage was originally to protect men's property and in modern times has served as an inadequate strategy to protect women and children from male abandonment. Legal marriage intends to force consequences (what I have called third-party intervention) on men who try to violate their promises and dishonorably abandon their responsibilities to women with whom they have shared love, sex, kindness, friendship. Even though the state always disadvantaged women, when it comes to marriage, there is some sense that married men do have some accountability to the women they have loved.

This, I think, is at the core of the desperate desire for relationship recognition that has spearheaded the campaign for gay marriage. Gay marriage does not so much protect the couple from the state as it protects the couple from each other. It is a third-party acknowledgment and recognition that people who have shared love have basic responsibilities toward each other. These responsibilities include having to go through some kind of process in order to change a relationship. Frankly, I think that this is a basic human responsibility and right to not be dehumanized by abandonment, shunning, pretending you have never loved. Legal marriage tries to create a framework, a process, a forced negotiation and forced communication that are inherent human responsibilities.

A second true motive, I believe, for galvanizing energy around gay marriage, is to force the state to legitimate the emotional life of the gay person as a balance to the deprivation of recognition created by the family. A father may not believe that his daughter is a person, but the state gives her the right to vote. In that tradition, the diminished gay person now has a new standing of status and recognition imposed by the state on the family. The state becomes an agent of third-party intervention, forcing the denying family into a mandated acknowledgment against their will, but transforming the social standard around them. Now individuals who are forced by law to recognize a gay marriage carry that new knowledge into their family. It is social pressure to change personal behavior.

In these ways, gay marriage is a strategy to prevent or dilute the tension created by withholding and shunning, both from family and from lover. It is this dynamic that I want to explore further.

Have you ever said "hello" to someone on the street and had them not reply? It creates tension. If the person stopped and said, "Hello, Sarah. How are you?", then we could experience human acknowledgment, the essential responsibility of people who know each other. But if they refuse that acknowledgment and instead choose shunning, they create a relationship of tension and conflict, which then needs to be resolved. In a way, this is the situation of gay people in America. We want the mutual relationship with the culture, but they refuse to respond. That refusal creates the tension, and it creates the urgent need on our parts to relieve the tension. Political movements are the product of the moment when the tension of exclusion or shunning is no longer bearable.

Let me restate this idea in other terms: people do things for reasons. Those reasons are located in earlier experiences. In that way, each moment is created by the previous moment. There is no behavior that is not in some way created by earlier experience. For this reason, the truth of any situation can be discovered in the sequence of events. What happened first? What followed? Awareness lies in identifying the core originating action and determining the sequence of its consequences. That's why people need to talk, so that the sequence of events can be understood. Too often we point to the consequences themselves without looking at the originating action that caused them. Gay people are upset; they are angry. Is this because they are inherently pathological? Or is the anger a result of someone else's originating action? An action that may be hard to describe or identify because it has been repeated so many times that it looks falsely neutral, or even nonexistent, when it is in fact the cause. Gay people are uncomfortable as a consequence of the exclusion. They are responding to the originating action of oppression, cruelty, dehumanization, diminishment, humiliation, deprivation of rights, however you wish to describe it. The cause is the shunning; shunning forces an urgent need for solution. Some people feel this solution to be gay marriage.

Back to the withholding person on the street. She is emblematic of the culture. The next time I see her, I ask, "Why are you angry, Culture? Lets sit down and talk it over." She refuses to answer and keeps walking. Her action *creates* a relationship far more intimate than the appropriate kindness would have created. Her action creates a relationship that is fraught and oppressive. It forces me to seek a solution, thereby deepening the connection between us, while she doesn't try to make things better. I am now forced to think about her, notice her, see what she is like, why she does what she does. In order to relieve the mysterious shunning, I must think like her in order to try to understand what she knows but will not communicate. I have to think on her terms in order to liberate myself from her shunning by ending it, to resolve it. As a result I know her better than she knows me. I know her ways. If I have humane empathy and she does not (as a consequence of privilege or trauma), I can see the justifications for her ways. I can see it from her point of view and my point of view. She thinks I don't have a point of view. I can see why she does what she does. This is both an expression of and source of love—the effort to understand. After being forced, by the oppression, to think about her so much, I develop a familiarity that makes her marriage acceptable to me while my homosexuality remains unacceptable to her.

Partially as a consequence of this one-sided identification, gay people increasingly wish to get married.

When we ask the culture why gay people must be constantly diminished, they often do not bother to answer at all. For example, I would like to know why literature with primary lesbian content can no longer be published with consistency in the United States. But I cannot get an answer. I would like to see a forum in the *New York Times Magazine* on this question, but there will not be one. If I ask someone, they don't respond. Charlie Rose will not raise it with his guests, even the lesbian ones. And they won't raise it either, or they wouldn't be on *Charlie Rose*. No play or movie will ask this question. It is a non-question because the people at stake are being treated as though we do not exist and have never existed. Lesbians are being treated as though we are not human and do not deserve representation—in literature or anywhere else. In fact we do not even have the right to discuss why we cannot have these things. This creates tension. The tension in turn creates an urgency for change. The silent exclusion creates the anxiety, which in turn creates the need to act for change; one causes the other. When people refuse to discuss why they are shunning you, when they give no reason and have no terms for reconciliation, it is because to actually talk about it would be to reveal their own behavior. And their power lies in the ability to command silence about their own behavior. They can only pretend to be neutral if the mechanics of the moment are not discussed. Once sequence and substance are laid out starkly, their responsibility is revealed. Hence, no conversation.

Right now, half of America believes that gay people are not human enough to deserve the right to get legally married. They have idealized ideas about themselves and about marriage, and distorted beliefs about us, what we're like and how much we can bear. What makes this moment more disturbing than twenty years ago is that, now, most of these people actually know gays and lesbians. More of us are out now, and so they hold their position with more viciousness, since it is aimed at human beings whose names they know.

They cling to this idealization of themselves for the same reason that more liberal people, who may support gay marriage, won't allow lesbian literature to exist. I believe it is because the dominant group (both the conservative and liberal wing) is deeply invested in seeing themselves, falsely, as neutrally objective and value free. If, in fact, other world-views were treated as equally legitimate, their sense of themselves as naturally superior would be dismantled. They don't want this. So, they maintain the exclusion and the silence around that exclusion as a way to falsely construct themselves as deserving of that power to shun. And this impulse is instinctive, not conscious. I believe that if there were an open, complex discussion of the exclusion, this answer would come to the forefront and that is why there is no such discussion. This is why, perhaps, my friend on the street won't discuss why she is angry. Because then her own cruelty would be revealed and she wouldn't be able to pretend neutrality. Shunners believe that they are doing nothing, or God's will, or maintaining the status quo, but actually their exclusion of us is very active, which is why it is so unbearable. If her own motivations would be visible, her actions might be exposed as unjustified. She, the culture, needs to maintain the refusal to discuss as a way to hide her own inadequacy.

Let's say the woman on the street does provide an answer. Perhaps she says, "It's God's will. It's not natural. Marriage is a covenant between a man and a woman," as her reason for keeping me out. Well, there is no God, so much for the legitimacy of that excuse. Or, let's say she explains her shunning by saying, "You broke into my apartment, stole my money, and used it to buy drugs. I will not speak to you again until you have three years of sobriety." If this drug thing is in fact what happened, my acquaintance is in the right. She has a clear, legitimate cause for her action. Her action is appropriate. It is justified. It is how I deserve to be treated by her. And furthermore, she has terms for reconciliation. This, too, is a basic human responsibility. If I comply with her terms, then we can sit down and negotiate. Of course, if I don't comply with her terms, she has the right to hold off contact until that changes. But to shun without terms is the definition of insanity. Once a person gives up on the possibility of human negotiation, they become apocalyptic. But, what if that drug answer, in fact, has no relationship to who I really am? I don't use drugs; I don't steal money; I have never committed the crime for which I am now being punished by silence. It is a false accusation. A smoke screen. She is mistaken. Or deliberately lying to cover up something else in her life that she can't face. It's her father who stole her money but she's blaming it on me. The burden, unfortunately, is now on me to reveal that she is mistaken, so that there can be relief for both of us. I don't have to be subjected to the pain of being on the receiving end of shunning, and she doesn't have to live with the poison of anger that is not rooted in the real. The consequence of her action on me is that I need the truth to become clarified so that she and I can both have better lives.

When gay people do get an answer as to why we are being excluded or separated, it is often not justified, not appropriate, and not how we deserve to be treated. It is most often a false accusation. These are some cruel justifications that I have heard. This is a true experience that I expressed in my novel, *Rat Bohemia*. I was on the way to my parents' house, but first I went to visit my friend Stan Leventhal. This story takes place in the 1980s or '90s. Stan was very sick. His apartment was a disaster; he was shaking, sweating. He gave me some books that he wanted me to have after he died. It was a stark, truthful moment. I think I was in my early thirties. I had already experienced many deaths. He shit in his pants. It was embarrassing and upsetting. I stayed with him longer than I anticipated. I arrived late at my parents' home. My sister was there with her boyfriend. I told my family why I was late. My mother said, "You only like men when they're dying. I had always hoped that you would grow up to be a productive person who was community-oriented but instead you put yourself in this mess."

My sister and her future husband sat there and said nothing.

There are many traumatic components in this experience. First, there is Stan's pain. His helplessness, his abandonment, his physical torture. Our open acknowledgment that he would soon die. The knowledge that his death was caused by societal neglect. The pain of his love for the book he gave me, *Jesus' Son,* by Denis Johnson. Second, there is the cumulative pain of experiencing the mass death of my friends, the helpless. Third, there is the trauma of having to explain this experience to my family—people whose privileges protected them from the true knowledge. Fourth, there is the lack of empathy or care from my family in the face of this experience. Fifth, my mother's insistence that my friends were not fully human. That they did not constitute a "community" and that, therefore, loving them did not constitute being connected to other humans. Her false accusation that I wish men to suffer and die because I am a homosexual. Sixth, there is the trauma of the erasure of my productivity and accomplishments. Seventh, the complicity of my sister and her future husband by remaining silent. The enjoyment of their privilege as a heterosexual couple in that room and their privileges of not having to experience the mass death of the young. Their decision to exploit those privileges instead of risking them to create a more humane family. Eighth, the false characterization of the truth of the AIDS crisis, "this mess," as something one chooses to experience. Not, in fact, something that one chooses to deny.

In this incident, my family members excluded me in a host of ways from their world of people whose feelings matter. They separated themselves from me. That is a punishment, and its consequences are brutal. The ability to be interactive with other human beings is the gift of life. Choosing to disconnect from others is either a pathological act of cruelty or a consequence of being on the receiving end of that cruelty. Withholding is never the positive choice. It is like the representative shunning woman on the street. Why would I want to be separated from her? To forever be punished for buying drugs I never bought? To forever be faced with silence when I say, "What did you do today?" To forever be denied the human experience of facing and dealing with problems with her, of the treasure of negotiation? To let her feel so badly and be so angry when there is no reason to feel so bad? To live forever on the receiving end of that unjustified anger?

I've been gay for a long time, thirty-five years this April, and I have met thousands of gay people around the world from all kinds of backgrounds, living in all kinds of conditions. Something I've noticed over and over again is that one of the most significant consequences of what we have endured is the creation of our various national and global subcultures. These subcultures are the highest stake in the gay marriage debate.

Some of us have CHOSEN to avoid the pain by living in subculture in order to minimize contact with the official culture and its people. When we make this choice, we don't socialize with them that much; we don't read their bad books; we try not to be subjected to their false ideas about us. Others of us have tried to transform them and failed. We've gone head-to-head with the glass ceilings, bad thinking, ignorance, cruelty and, then, if we're defeated, we are then *forced* back into subculture simply because they won't let us into the big world. We have commitment ceremonies and publish with marginal presses.

There is also the third intention: choosing to live in the subculture as a place to prepare to force change. And this is where so many gay people of my generation have lived. Viewing our subcultural commitments as a way of strengthening ourselves for the task ahead of changing the big structures so that we can live inside them, alongside straight people, without being distorted by them. That is the most utopian, most difficult, and yet most inspiring option. So far, it has not been successful.

The desire for gay marriage is, in many ways, a refusal of all of those subcultural positions. For in some ways, gay marriage is a sign of spiritual exhaustion. It is a way to get out of the trenches, the white flag of surrender that can bring the tired soldier to a hot shower and a bowl of gruel.

So now I see gay and straight people getting married and, as a consequence, I look at their relationships. These are supposed to be good relationships that enhance the world—that's why the world is cheering them on, right? But, I see many relationships that frighten me. One thing I have seen is talented, exceptional people hooking up with simple, more limited people so that the relationship can be built entirely around the centrality of the more gifted partner. This upsets me. I find it disappointing and somewhat monstrous. I also see people who can stay together because the connection is superficial; they fear a depth of understanding. Some of them have been traumatized and truly reaching another person triggers, falsely, fear of violation. I see many relationships that are boring, not fun, repetitive. Is this truly what these people would want given a state of nature? And will they produce follow-the-leader children, who will in turn make the rest of us miserable?

So little is right about how we live today, and relationships are the microcosm of the society. Stalin noticed that "the family is the building block of Socialism," and he was right. Relationships keep the social order, but what about when the social order sucks? When it is social imperative, convenience, and shallowness that cement the bond, do we have to say "Mazel Tov"? I hate to open up this can of worms, but do destructive relationships and their consequential impact on those around them deserve a party? George Bush's marriage reinforced and protected his destroying other people's lives everyday. Many relationships allow people to stay cruel, dishonest and cause havoc and pain. We'd be better off if these were not rewarded simply for existing.

Conversely, I see breakups that never should have happened. That are wrong, symptoms of mental illness, alcoholic behavior, untreated post-traumatic stress. I have also experienced and witnessed lesbian breakups rooted in the devaluation of one partner from outside the relationship, and the power of suggestion on the other, similarly devalued partner. Once individuals learn that no one cares how their lover is treated and also that no one cares how they themselves behave, they too can act out their fear and anger on the same person being scapegoated by the culture, the person before them. If there was gay marriage, perhaps this would be somewhat reduced. That woman shunning me on the street? If she were my legal wife, she wouldn't be able to just stop speaking to me one day; she'd have to negotiate something, say a few sentences. The law would mandate it. The law would care, and I think that would be a good thing.

If gay people know that the law cares about how they treat their lover, perhaps they would be slightly kinder. If they felt that their lover was considered to be a human, and not lesser than, perhaps they would be able to negotiate and express instead of just destroy. If gay marriage would make her have to "show cause," I am for it.

I recently had a dinner party at my house with four friends from San Francisco. Wine collectors. On bottle four, one of them, Alice Hill, said, "Gay marriage is like abortion. Whatever you think of it, you have to have the right." Okay, I can go along with that. But my enthusiasm ends there. What I really want is for the shunning to end so I can stop thinking about how I have to change myself to make the shunning stop when I know it's unjustified in the first place. I want to see you on the street and say, "How are you?" and have you smile and let me know. I want my books to be equal to your books. I want my death to be equal to your death. I want my feelings to be equal to your feelings and my place in the family to be equal to yours. And when you're mad about something, I want it to be for real reasons that can be articulated, and then I want us to sit down and solve them together. If I had these things, I would not need gay marriage.

TO BE REAL

"The first step in liquidating a people is to erase its memory. Destroy its books, its culture, its history. Then have somebody write new books, manufacture a new culture, invent a new history. Before long the nation will begin to forget what it is and what it was. The world around will forget even faster."

—Milan Kundera

Now I want to discuss prime time shunning: the exclusion of lesbians from culture. Not being represented in a media culture puts one at a gross disadvantage. I want to share some experiences and perceptions with how the lack of mainstream, exterior authentic representation, reinforces the dehumanization of gay people within the family structure. I want to especially share with you literally *how* the exclusion of lesbian content replicates the structures of scapegoating, victimization, false accusations, and shunning. By examining this, you can understand the materiality of this on-going, backstage phenomenon.

If you have no family, and you have no society, often the only thing you have is a vision of a different world. That's why so many alienated people live in the movies, books, plays, television. Because I am an artist, my relationship to these images is as a consumer and a producer. I sit in my room, and I get to have my say, to grapple with the questions that matter to me, to create new paradigms. It's my calling. It's absorbing, and a great freedom is there—the freedom to *potentially* exist.

But in order to *actually* exist, the work must leave my room. From this necessity, a new question arises, that of *materiality*. What good is it to make work that no one else sees? Of course, there are historical swings to these representational questions. At times, women represent 12 percent of all playwrights whose work gets produced in a given season. At other times, women represent 7 percent. You know, it ebbs and ebbs.

I'm working with a wonderful actress, a great lady of the stage. She has asked me to write a play for her and we've done the work, made something really special and it's ready for the world. No takers. She calls me:

"How can this be? How can the play be any good if nobody wants it?"

"Honey," I say. "Plays don't get done because they're good."

There is still no lesbian play in the American repertoire, and I promise that that is not because all the men are better writers.

Back to the drawing board.

Some years back a young white gay man from a wealthy family, who doesn't work and who has a prestigious graduate school degree (this describes so many people that saying so implicates no one), showed me a play. I read it and I told him that the women characters were not real. But I added that I was sure that no one would care but me. He showed it to the gay male literary manager at a theater and told him he was worried about the female characters.

"You're a gay man," the literary manager told him. "Don't worry about that. It's not your area of interest."

A year later the play got produced and there were two very different kinds of responses. A black female critic (there was only one so you know who she is) said that the writing was predictable because the Asian and female characters were condescended to. A white gay male critic (there are so many to choose from, it's dizzying) said that the play is brilliant.

I ponder this discrepancy.

What does "brilliant" mean?

Is it true that if a man creates characters out of people who have fewer rights than he does, and these characters are not fully human, in a context where real people who are just like those characters cannot get their plays produced, does that mean he is a "predictable" (predictable in his dehuman-ization of the less powerful) writer or a "brilliant" one? Does white gay male critic #5 care, or even consider, whether or not people unlike himself are fully drawn? And would he know if they were? Is the play "brilliant" because the people in question don't matter or brilliant because the critic doesn't know anyone like them well enough to see how distorted their representations are?

I'm of the school of thought that says that a good writer writes complex characters. They have language and a structure that comes organically from the emotions at the core of the piece. They are grappling with something that matters. And the values of the piece are not rooted in maintaining the supremacy of the dominant. That last one is the killer.

After over three decades as a working artist in a variety of forms, it has become clear to me that there is no relationship between quality and reward. Sometimes good work gets rewarded, but not because it is good. That's just a coincidence.

Let's face it, people think that the system works if it works for them. If artwork was fairly evaluated on its merit instead of demographic or point of view, an entirely different cast of characters would be reaping rewards. The rewarded get what they get because they're, for example, white, but they think they're just better. They confound demographic (accident of birth) and quality. And whenever one person outside the box manages to be an exception, they insist it's because she's black. "They gave it to her because she's black" is something you hear all the time. "They needed a woman." But the truth is that those guys get it BECAUSE they are white. Not because of the depth and breadth of their Asian and female characters.

And lesbian literature? Oy vey. Now here's a long story. The battle for lesbian representation in American publishing is more complex than the Battle of Bulge. And more bloody. Occasionally, books pop up on the radar every few decades, even big sellers like the 1950s hit *The Price of Salt* by "Claire Morgan" (the pseudonymously frightened Patricia Highsmith). Skip a few years to *Rubyfruit Jungle,* published in 1973. After that, the only overtly lesbian protagonists by lesbian authors to be allowed on mainstream America's bookshelves were from Britain. Since the British mainstream publishers published Jeanette Winterson and Sarah Waters in the first place, marketed them like regular people, reviewed them in regular places as though they were full human beings, rewarded their labors, made films out of their books, the U.S. presses decided that they were worthy of republication. But since no lesbian writer with lesbian content could be treated the same way here, none were able to achieve the same level of currency that Winterson and Waters have been able to achieve. So they get re-published here, occupying the American shelf space for quality lesbian fiction because they have already achieved an acclaim that we are not allowed to have. Basically, as Urvashi Vaid has said, in America "lesbian content is the kiss of death."

My first lesbian characters were Harriet the Spy and Anne Frank. In high school in New York City in 1974, I went to the Oscar Wilde Memorial Bookshop and bought and read *Sappho Was A Right-On Woman* by Sydney Abbott and Barbara Love. In college in 1977, I read *Rubyfruit Jungle*, the edition from Daughters Incorporated. The first lesbian reading I ever went to was in 1979 by Joan Larkin, Susan Sherman, and Honor Moore. I was very inspired by the pioneer generation in New York City—the people already on the scene when I came into it—Audre Lorde, Adrienne Rich, Irena Klepfisz. I admired their intellectual prowess and personalized their message, feeling that they wanted me to be a moral person. I still feel this way about them. Many of the decisions I've made in my writing and in how I've handled my career have been determined by this feeling of having to live up to them. Audre was my teacher at Hunter College; she's been dead for years. I met Adrienne Rich once for five minutes. Irena and I occasionally meet at demonstrations. Yet, I made them into a lineage or an ancestry and imagined that they had expectations of me. I imagined that they were raising me to practice democratic principles of community-building and to apply them to the literary community, which to me means returning phone calls, responding honestly to people's work, being available, helping people who have less access, maintaining integrity about lesbian content, always knowing that there are some things that are more important than money. Keeping my promises. With these kinds of ideas, I made them into my ancestors.

Grace Paley, another one of these people I pretend is watching me, says that writers choose their themes when we are very young and stick with them our whole lives. One of my main themes is creating the lesbian life as an organic part of American literature. This has forced me since my first novel was published when I was twenty-five—twenty-six years ago—to constantly look at the reality of what we are living and translate it into an artful representation or, in some of my books, a representational art object.

What are the stakes in this? Why is having authentic lesbian content excluded from mainstream representation reinforcing shunning and oppression in gay people's daily lives? The key answer is POWER. Truthful lesbian representations teach straight people, through some trickle down theory, to be kinder to gay people. But it's not just that. With lesbian representations, lesbians can see truthful depictions of themselves and thereby realize that they are human. But it's not just that either. Far more important is the daily material behavior of the people who create popular culture, people constructing global ideas about kindness and beauty behind the scenes. These influential people determine whose work will be seen, what paradigms will dominate and become normalized, who will be able to earn a living, what kinds of opportunities artists will have to develop. They determine who will feel right and who will feel wrong. Remember, what gets seen has almost no relationship to what is created. What is created is what is expressed; what is seen is what is selected.

Let me give you an example. This story takes place in 2003. I am working on a musical adaptation of my novel, *Shimmer*. My collaborators are the lyricist Michael Korie, who was the lyricist for the Broadway musical *Grey Gardens*, and a character in the story of the transformation of my novel *People In Trouble* into the musical *Rent* (see my book *Stagestruck: Theater, AIDS and the Marketing of Gay America*, 1998), a composer we will call Notorious P.I.G., and a director/producer we will call Manny Brice. We had been working for years. At the center of the musical is a lesbian romance. Not only is there no authentic lesbian play in the American canon (*The Children's Hour's* tragic homosexual narrative does not count), but also there has NEVER been a real lesbian protagonist in any American musical. So this content is exciting, important, and difficult. Furthermore, the piece is about the McCarthyite mentality and takes place against the backdrop of the blacklist. The issues of scapegoating and exclusion and silencing are at the core of the work itself.

We've been having a series of workshops and Manny is heavily dramaturging the piece. I take every one of his notes. Every line of the musical's book is exactly the way he wants it to be. Every word. We have a final read-through of the script at his apartment. He changes one line. Now we're ready for a workshop with actors.

Casting the central role of the bi-sexual white woman married to the black playwright and sleeping with the young lesbian neighbor is crucial. Casting for lesbian roles is a complicated and difficult process. I currently have a number of plays with lesbian protagonists in "development" around the country. This means that the plays are having readings, staged readings, and workshops in a variety of venues that will hopefully result in productions. While laborious and anxiety-provoking, this process has given me the opportunity to hear the same plays be presented by a wide range of actors working in very different circumstances. I've heard plays read by regional repertory companies in small cities, by A-level New York stage actresses, by students in various collegiate theater departments, and by neophyte companies. I've seen the same part read by a twenty-five-year old ingénue from a regional conservatory, and an over-fifty-years-on-stage New York theater veteran.

I have to say that I am lucky. I have been able to work with some great stage artists, and with many good ones. But strangely, the one thing that most of them share is an inability to play a lesbian convincingly on stage. I've worked with gifted actresses who can easily transform themselves into full human beings whom they have never been. I've worked with a robust young woman who brilliantly played a paraplegic, a

Texas Southern Baptist who won great acclaim playing a Jewish princess, a young Asian woman of enormous range who fully inhabited a white southern gossip. I've worked with actresses who have played every accent, age, class, and point of view. And yet, overwhelmingly, most of them have no idea of how to play a lesbian.

The first question is WHY? The obvious reason is there is no lesbian play in the American repertoire. There is no play, from a lesbian perspective, with openly gay female protagonists that has been broadly produced in regional theaters, with a major production in New York. As a result, there is no standard lesbian text used in scene work in acting schools. And so, there is no unifying theatrical reference point from which heterosexual actresses can learn. So, when straight actresses come to a play that is fully from a lesbian perspective, they are working with something that they have not only never worked with before but have never even seen performed. Or heard about it being performed. The producers have never experienced producing such a play, and the directors have no experience directing them. Everyone is starting from scratch. Except the writer. Most lesbian writers working with primary lesbian content for the stage have been channeled into performance or performative-styled live work. This work uses direct address, is often solo, or has the writer perform in the piece, or has a more vaudeville or performance art style. It is taken less seriously than the blue-chip form of conventional "play" in which the playwright asserts the authority of creating a contained universe occupied by multiple characters. People who don't have full citizenship are encouraged into performance art instead of plays because it occupies the kind of lighter side of entertainment; historically Jews and blacks were channeled into this form of entertainment through stand-up comedy. Now gay and lesbian people and Latino people are. The more respected, more rewarded, and more authoritative form of theatre is still restricted to men, and generally white men.

There are some lesbian actresses, but it is not a profession friendly to homosexual women. Most of the gay women in the theater are stage managers, casting directors, and other people working behind the scenes. Those actresses who, through talent and commitment and sometimes the casting couch, have survived, are often afraid to play gay parts. They worry that, once seen as gay, they will never be cast as straight again. To spend one's career playing tomboys, next-door neighbors, virgins and freaks is not any gifted actor's dream. So, the task generally falls to heterosexual women, asked to transform into and embody a social and erotic reality that they've never fully seen represented. Interestingly, these actresses often make the same mistakes. Over and over I've seen straight actresses try their best to show emotional and erotic connection with other women on stage, only to have the real lesbians in the audience complain after that "they looked like straight women playing dykes." I find myself sitting in theaters wincing at absolutely unconvincing kissing scenes, painfully inept attempts to portray physical intimacy, and misguided gestures toward romantic love.

The most frequent mistake that actresses playing couples make is that they try to establish some kind of outward sign of erotic intimacy by touching each other frequently during the presentation. Regularly, two actresses sitting next to each other, who are playing a couple, will over the course of the reading, turn closer and closer to each other in their chairs until they are facing each other and not the audience. This does not read as erotic partners; it reads as space invasion. Then, they tend to touch each other too much, and in a kind of petting gesture—usually on the arm or back. It looks like they are compulsively brushing lint off the other's sweater. If theater professionals were experienced with lesbian representation, the director would immediately put an end to this. But how is anyone to know? Erotic tension is defined by distance and deliberate purposeful physical contact so that the impulse to touch is ever present. As one of my favorite actresses, and one of the few who can play gay convincingly, Jenny Bacon, put it, "She has to *want* me to touch her." Without the discernment of desire, they end up cloying and clawing in a manner that dilutes all possible erotic power.

Even if the over-pawing is brought to an end, most heterosexual actresses don't seem to know where to put their hands when the time for touch is right. Over and over again I see arms go around shoulders. That's how friends hold each other, not lovers. If we are in an extended workshop, over the course of days, and I have a chance to get to know the actors and to speak to them casually, I try to bring it up. The ideal way to show erotic power and possession is for one woman to put her arm around the other's *waist*. To hook her hand into the curve of the other's body. This is a lesbian, sexual touch, not the way friends hold each other in greeting.

Beyond physicality, there are other attributes that let an actress read as *lesbian* convincingly on stage. Interestingly, one actress who has repeatedly successfully played lesbian characters is Jessica Hecht. She appeared in Diana Son's *Stop Kiss*, a play by a non-lesbian woman about two straight women whose friendship results in a romantic kiss, for which they are brutally gay-bashed. Then, Hecht played an on-going lesbian character on the TV show FRIENDS. When she has read the openly lesbian leads for my plays, I saw in person why she is so persuasive playing lesbians. She listens. Intensely. She gives so much attention to the other people on stage that when the other person is cast as her female lover, Hecht's ability to listen reads erotically. Listening reveals a kind of positive submission, a generous investment in the other. And this is something rarely seen on stage between two female characters who are not related.

Erotic interest is a kind of light. And when it is returned, the whole theater is illuminated. This can't be achieved through substitution, pretending that the woman before you is a man. It has to be found organically between the two actresses, and what is the best way for this to be achieved? Through knowledge, awareness, and talent. In other words, through craft. And how is craft learned? Through experience. Hopefully, as the world changes, lesbian plays will become an organic part of the American theater, and only then will actresses have the chance to study and learn how to fully inhabit these characters.

So these were the obstacles facing the casting of *Shimmer*. Now with an artistic team of three gay men and me, you can imagine which one of us was preoccupied with these questions. The men thought that whoever we had was fine. Good actresses kept coming in and having NO IDEA how to play the relationship. But only I seemed to notice. How could the guys notice? They'd never experienced it personally and, since it had never been represented, they had no idea what it would look like if two women lovers were alone in a room. We went through a number of interesting actresses but none of them could get it. I kept saying, "This isn't right," but no one felt the concern that I did.

Finally, Michael Mayer recommended an actress to me named Sharon Scruggs who was at the time understudying his production of *Thoroughly Modern Millie* on Broadway. She came in and she was fantastic. She was intelligent, sexy, musical, seductive. She could play all the subtext that none of the other women could figure out. Like Jessica and Jenny, she transcended the category. Well, this changed the entire piece. For the first time, the lesbian sexuality was central to the performance in the way that it was intended to be. The whole work changed and came alive. It was exciting. Thrilling. After the reading the artistic team went upstairs to have our meeting. I was so happy. I thought that now that the guys had seen how it was supposed to be, they would praise me. We came into Manny's office, closed the door, and P.I.G. said:

"Sarah, you get titillated by watching sexy actresses play lesbian scenes, but I find it tedious. And no one from Iowa is going to want to pay $90 to see that."

I was so shocked and so blindsided that my head started spinning. I did not know what to say. I looked around at the other men, expecting them to explode with anger at Piggy. But they didn't say a word. They just sat there as though this kind of behavior was fine. The rest of the meeting was a whirl for me. I felt so terrible, so humiliated to be treated that way. Later, when I got home, I realized that Piggy had accused me of being a homosexual and of being a writer. Why was he able to make those two things sound so disgusting? That night the phone rang; it was Manny. Piggy was refusing to complete the second half of the score unless we brought in one of the other men from the team to rewrite the book. This was an adaptation of MY NOVEL, with a book that

Manny himself had micro-managed. Of course I refused, and of course I was so upset. The sexism was the originating action, me being upset was the consequence of Piggy and Manny's humiliating behavior. Now I was devastated. I said "no." I realize now how Piggy used shunning, by not calling me and talking to me himself, but creating an exclusive structure of deflection from which to scapegoat without the possibility of conversation. I told Manny that I would not agree to that and that he was wrong to even be calling me with such a thing.

He responded, "Sarah, I know it's hard for you to hear, but you can't write."

I got off the phone, overwhelmed by the series of assaults. As it sank in, I became angrier and angrier. As I began to process the dishonest mindfuck that I was being subjected to, I started to get some clarity about how I was being scapegoated. I phoned Manny back. Of course he put his shunning mechanism into place by screening his calls and refusing to pick up the phone. This after years of working together on the project and after he approved the script. I left a very upset message. If he had not been shunning and withholding, we could have discussed exactly what was really going on here. They were panicking about the lesbian content and pretending that I "can't write." How sleazy can you get? And how clichéd? If he had negotiated and been interactive, the truth would have had to be faced, but by shunning it could be repressed.

I phoned my dear friend Marion McClinton, the great stage director who had directed my play about Carson Mc-Cullers and who was one of August Wilson's primary collaborators. Marion is black, so when these kinds of scapegoating situations emerge, he can always see clearly what is really going on. When I got to the part where Manny said, "I know it's hard for you to hear, but you can't write," Marion started laughing.

"He played that old game? That is so tired."

I e-mailed Piggy and asked for the two of us to get together to talk. He refused. Of course. I was the less powerful one and so he, a gay man, was shunning me. If he had a human face-to-face conversation with me about what was going on, his prejudices, and sense of supremacy might be deflated. There was no reason for him to deal with things truthfully—the silence of the other men had made clear to him that he could treat me any way he wanted to. I had no power. I, and lesbian representation, had no currency and didn't matter. He has, to this day, continued the shunning, refusing to sit down with me and resolve this experience.

The happy ending is that Michael Korie apologized to me for standing by and letting this cruelty be enacted. He and I took the piece to Anthony Davis, a well-respected innovative composer, who is also black. Like Marion, when we told him the story, he laughed with recognition. He could spot that type of brutality a mile away. Now Anthony is composing the piece.

Look at the material difference between Piggy's experience and mine. He gets to act out homophobic cruelty that he himself has experienced, but he gets to revictimize by choosing an even more vulnerable target, a gay woman. He got to extend the cruelty of the culture. Doing this helps him feel normal, superior, and neutral in relationship to me, who is created as someone whose life does not deserve to be seen or expressed. And he calls on the people of Iowa as the justification for his own visceral rejection of overt lesbian content. He counts on patriarchy, the old boys' network, to empower him to humiliate me. And then he and Manny use the age old last drawer desperate justification. It's not that they are sick with prejudice. It's that they are good, and I am bad. It's the girl who, coincidentally, happens to be the bad writer. Obviously. Suddenly, after nine books, ten plays, a Guggenheim, Fulbright, the list could go on, I can't write. They construct themselves as superior to me, even though I actually have more accomplishments. They rely on every sick cruel trick of supremacy and then Piggy hides behind e-mail and phone machines to avoid taking responsibility for his actions.

Telling the story here is a *consequence* of the shunning, the withholding expressed by him hiding behind e-mail and phone machines. If he would negotiate and be interactive, I would have other alternatives. As it stands, writing this is my only alternative. What's fascinating about shunning is that people are so distorted by their own sense of supremacy that they actually believe that you will and should follow their command of silence. It's both bizarre and creates a lot of pain in conflicts that simple negotiating could resolve.

Let me say clearly that trying to publish lesbian novels and get lesbian plays produced in this era means encountering this kind of distorted assaultive shunning and cruelty on a regular basis. At least once a week some kind of devaluative experience takes place. Someone acts disrespectfully, disregards my level of merit and achievement, diminishes something of value, because the lesbian content of the work removes any currency that my accomplishments might otherwise create. And lest you feel compelled to try to excuse or justify this, there is no other lesbian writer working in these forms (novels with lesbian protagonists, multi-character stage plays with lesbian point of view) who is faring any better. There is no one else who because of more talent, a more user-friendly personality, better connections, a trust fund, or an Ivy League degree has been able to get lesbian content novels and plays at the appropriate levels of presentation and recognition. Even great, openly lesbian writers like Paula Vogel, who won a well-deserved Pulitzer Prize for *How I*

Learned To Drive, have not been able to have success with a work with serious multi-character dramatic universes with overt primary lesbian content. Where we are allowed to function in theatre is with closeted or coded work and performative or solo theater pieces. None of this is because of the quality of the artistic achievement, nor is it because of the marketplace and people in Iowa. I have learned from repeated experience that it is entirely because of the individuals with the power of selection, their practice of devaluing who we are, our consequential lack of power and social currency, and the ease with which people feel free to extend the shunning they have observed us experience in every other institution of life.

What is so sinister is that just as this structure keeps complex lesbian content out of mainstream culture, its absence is then experienced, I think subconsciously, by perpetrators in the private sphere as justification for their actions. When a person scapegoats a gay family member, there is no big movie, book, or play creating a cultural status quo telling them not to. The reason for this is that the people with power behind the scenes in art and entertainment behave exactly the same way that people with power do in the private sphere. The shunning is dynamic and mutually reinforcing.

The history of lesbian literature is a bit more complex than the stage because in book publishing we did break through during the 1990s and have now lost those advances. In theater, the breakthrough still has not occurred. Because it takes so much personal strength to have primary lesbian content in this era, the writers who persevere need some sense of historical context to be able to understand what is happening to us right now and why. Oppression is both informative about the powerful other and infantilizing about the self. We have a very sophisticated understanding of the structures that keep oppression in place. We understand the dominant cultural mind and how it is constructed while they still don't even know that their power *is* constructed. We are experts on them. But no one is expert on us.

Lesbian publishing became established in the 1970s by pioneers like Wendy Cadden, June Arnold, Joan Larkin, and Barbara Grier, with presses like Out and Out Press, Daughters Inc., and Diana Press and later Persephone and Crossing Press, Naiad and Firebrand, Cleis and Seal. Collectively, the feminist publishing movement produced excellent work by superior writers. Work that was as technically advanced as any competitive writer in the marketplace and work that was extremely meaningful to its readers, far beyond the impact of most mainstream writers on their readers. The challenge then moved from the already difficult act of getting these works into print to the next, far more difficult step. Namely, to have our most talented and achieved writers and works of art recognized on the basis of their merit without having to compromise the primacy of the lesbian characters. This is the challenge that we still face.

The one thing that has substantially changed in the publishing world is that a writer can be openly lesbian personally and still be accepted as an American writer as long as she produces some work with no primary lesbian content. So, the current state of affairs is that books where the lesbian content is coded, sub-textual, involved with secondary characters or sub-plots, written in what is called "lesbian sensibility" or featuring strong women characters with ambiguous sexualities are considered "well written." Books in which the protagonist is a lesbian in the first and last chapter? These books are not "well written." They are considered to not deserve to be part of American fiction because the lives that they depict are not acceptable lives. Books with primary lesbian characters are diminished and demeaned because the prejudice and stigma against the characters results in a series of institutionalized lies. Namely that the books are "about homosexuality," are "political, not literary," and are all alike. This results in an institutionalized quota system in which books with primary lesbian characters are only compared to each other, only compete against each other, and are never ever placed in the spectrum of American fiction. Even magazines practice this censorship. If the *New Yorker* or the *Atlantic* or their ilk have published fiction by openly lesbian American authors with primary lesbian content, it's escaped me.

As the obvious merit and ability of lesbian writers became clearer, one of the goals of the lesbian publishing movement became to have our best work accepted by the widest range of American readers. Unfortunately, the opposite has happened. Before the advent of niche marketing in 1992, people wrote books with primary lesbian and gay characters because they had to. They were artistically and ethically compelled to this decision despite the almost certain knowledge that it would prohibit them from ever being able to earn a living. They were speaking to the world from a place of truth. Once people began to perceive of a gay market, they wrote book proposals to develop books purposefully for that market, books that were as superficial as meaningless books that straight people were sold, but with a gay lilt. So rather than our best work and our best talents being recognized and integrated into American literature, the publishing industry bombarded our own community with junk books such as *The Gay Hair Book* which then dominated the shelves of gay book stores, when there were still many gay book stores. Simultaneously, we were making no progress in getting our quality lesbian literature out to the general public.

There was a brief window between approximately 1986

and 1992 when publishing started to open up to lesbian literature. Due to pioneering editors like Carole DeSanti, (who, I believe, has since abandoned lesbian fiction), writers like Carole Maso, Jacqueline Woodson, Jane DeLynn, Patricia Powell, Jennifer Levin, Carol Anshaw and many others were able to publish adult novels with primary lesbian content in mainstream houses at the same time. Some years there would be five to eight lesbian novels published in a given season. However, once niche marketing was put into play, these expansive, gifted writers had their books literally moved from the "Literature" sections of chain stores to the newly created "Gay and Lesbian" sections, usually in the back of a top floor of Barnes and Noble somewhere behind the potted plants. In this way, our best literature was guaranteed marginalization, while work by lesbians with no lesbian content came to occupy the public "gay" space and got treated as American literature.

Interestingly, the families of gays and lesbians behave the same way in the marketplace as they do in the halls of justice. Absent. Just as they do not fight for full inclusion into the society of their gay family members, they do not purchase or consume artworks that come from the cultural point of view of their gay family members. Lesbian novels are just as overlooked or ignored or demeaned as every other part of our lives.

Now, this being America, it is really shocking to find out

that the one thing more powerful than money is homophobia. Because, of course, all these publishers could make more money if they presented this literature in a more general way. And many of these lesbian books sold more copies than books by straights. But, fascinating and devastating as it may be, the publishing industry has shown no interest in breaking open the niche market. The shunning of artworks and artists who have enough integrity to be consistently out in our work is almost complete. It absolutely reflects the lived reality we experience in relation to other social institutions. I want to explore why and how these obstacles are kept in place and then look at what we can do to change them.

First of all, agents, editors, publishers, magazine editors, publicists, and marketers are in the social role of cultural administrators. They don't create ideas; they select and package them. That is just a fact. But when you are in an era of immense social repression, as we are in, cultural administrators take on a crucial role. They can either resist and mitigate the new order or they can pander to and implement it. What I have seen in the last years is that the general mood of agents and editors is that, yes, indeed, books with primary lesbian content are not good books, not well written books and are in and of themselves deficient by nature. A world view that is very consistent with what we're seeing on the evening news and in the realm of the family.

"Throw in a murder," is a suggestion that more than one

publishing professional has suggested to more than one superb, but newly unpublishable writer. "Just throw in a murder. Make it an erotic thriller." I would point out that my colleagues with coded, euphemistic, subtextual, or secondary lesbian content were not being told to throw in a murder. "If only you had written *After Delores* ten years later," one of them said to me. "You would be rich." In other words, in the view of almost every lesbian agent or editor that I have spoken to, the reason that no novel with primary lesbian characters since *Rubyfruit Jungle* has been accepted as fully American is because something is wrong with the books. All of them. They are all deficient. And they all need to be changed. They all need to have a murder. Because lesbianism is not literary. Our lives are not poetry; they are not dramatic; they are not interesting; they have no merit. The projection of shame is overwhelming. It is sad and pathetic. But we see it everywhere.

Queer editors of national gay magazines put straight people on the covers all the time. Can you imagine Al Jolson on the cover of *Ebony* saying what it's like to work in blackface? Lesbian editors and agents are no more advanced in their self-esteem than anyone else, and they work in isolating, grueling straight corporate environments. If you're in an office sixty hours a week, you can't have any idea of what is really going on out there, can you? Celebrities who came out after they got famous or made it with work that was closeted are better than ones who have always been out. That's what the gay and straight press hammer at us everyday. A famous cover story in *Entertainment Weekly* of gay people in the business featured sixteen photographs of key players in the gay entertainment boom. The only one who had started his career out of the closet was RuPaul. It is the Jody Foster syndrome. We are dependent on gay people in cultural administration positions to have the kind of self-esteem and vision and self-love and personal integration to see through these lies, that many of them cannot, do not, and will not have. And so the vision has to come from us.

So now, what is to be done?

As in all areas, the answer lies in third-party intervention.

The first step is that agents and authors with clout need to put the issues on the table with the publishers and producers. I have had a lot of experience with agents (both theatrical and literary) who will acknowledge privately that work is being diminished for its lesbian content but who will not sit down with the selectors and say so. They keep the information as the author's private burden. In publishing, most editors have never acquired a novel by an openly lesbian writer with primary lesbian content. Most have NEVER, in their entire careers, bid on such a novel. Yet, if you ask them directly, they would claim that they themselves are not prejudiced and would, theoretically, be open to publishing such a novel. It's just that no novel that they like has ever come along. If anyone with access would ask the right questions, the next obvious place to go in the conversation is to ask these liberal, progressive, powerful editors the following question:

Why is it that nothing that lesbian writers express corresponds with what you think should be heard?

It's a profound question. And a difficult one. All of these editors have published numerous books by straight and closeted people that have tanked. They have published numerous books that don't matter and sold no copies. Why would they choose those over lesbian books with dynamic content and loyal readers? Obviously, something is at play that is more pressing than sales.

Now rethink this question in the context of the issues raised by this book. The editors grew up in families where, to greater or lesser degree, the message of heterosexual supremacy was made clear. A message that is not true, but is enforced. Whether they are straight or gay, they left their families for an educational system that emphasized heterosexual supremacy. They live in a country whose laws emphasize heterosexual supremacy. They watch movies, plays, and television that pathologize gay people and elevate straight people, even though in truth straight people are not superior. In every arena of life, they have seen gay people be FALSELY diminished and shunned. They work in an industry where lesbian women have achieved some power and influence, in

part, by excluding lesbian content from American letters. Socially, politically, representationally, and personally they have
seen gay women who are out in their work be excluded and
demeaned. Now they receive a novel that reflects this experience of being shunned. What do they do with it?

Shun it!

They are looking for a novel that will not reflect the lived
experience of its author. They simply repeat and replicate
the systems of exclusion and scapegoating that they have
been raised with because the fact is that NOTHING a lesbian has to say authentically about her life would be acceptable for normative positioning within publishing. For her to
speak from a place of authority would not be normal. Only
for her to be shunned would be normal. And since book
publishing is about being normal, it is restricted to people
who are normal.

Straight authors with big guns in house could make a big
difference with all of this. For example, Stephen King, Terry
McMillan, and Amy Tan could transform the situation. Imagine them on subway ads, smiling, and the caption saying, "We
read gay and lesbian books. Lesbian books are part of American literature." Come on Oprah. Pick a novel with an openly
lesbian writer and a lesbian protagonist. YOU CAN DO IT.
PEN AMERICAN CENTER supports repressed writers in
other countries. What about here? And STOP NICHE
MARKETING. Gay books need to be mixed advertised

with straight writers of the same level of merit, even if they have more stature due to the privileging of heterosexual content. These ads should run in mainstream publications. Gay authors and straight authors should be toured together. The publishers need to encourage comparisons to writers with similar aesthetic concerns, not just other gay work. I know that my playwriting is closest aesthetically to the work of Donald Margulies and Jon Robin Baitz, but because of my content, no one would ever make that comparison. My novels are closest to Paul Auster and Philip Roth, but I've spent my life being compared to other dykes. If magazines are clearly operating with quota systems for work with lesbian content, the publishers need to directly address this issue with the book review assignment editors. Two or ten books by lesbian authors can appear on the same list at any given house if they are treated like books. I recently was told by an openly lesbian editor at a progressive house that she couldn't even look at this manuscript because she had "too many LGBT books in the pipeline." Does anyone ever refuse to consider a manuscript because they have too many heterosexual books in the pipeline? To make us compete against each other is ridiculous.

It is niche marketing that keeps straight people from fully accessing gay and lesbian material. Stop pre-ordaining limited audiences for our literature. White people read books by black authors; Christians read books by Jews. Straight people can read books and see plays about lesbians. They'll get used to it. Publishers need to openly address with magazines, newspapers, funding organizations, awards boards, curatorial spaces like PEN, writers workshops, publishing institutes, etc., that they know that author X is as talented as any straight person publishing today and that this publisher expects her books to be treated in that manner. And when the institutions do exclude and marginalize, the publishers have to be ready to call and address that marginalization. You may think that this sounds like a lot. But it is not. It is a very easy process once you get used to it. And in the long run, it will pay off in expanding market possibilities so that our most talented writers are not forced, psychologically and financially, into the world of acceptable sub-text. If this does not happen, we will end up with generations of writers with no place to go, client lists that cannot make money, and an increasingly narrow range of voices presented in an increasingly censorious cultural field.

This exclusion is dynamic with the way lesbians are treated in the public and private spheres and becomes a propaganda message of silent endorsement to homophobic family members as they go about their day.

CONCLUSION

Facing Challenging Ideas

When Ronald Reagan was elected president in 1980, he allowed the formerly fringe Christian Right to move their agenda, which was called "The Family Protection Act," center stage. This coalition began to push through a wide array of anti-abortion restrictions on local and national levels. One of these efforts was a federal bill called The Human Life Statute, which would have outlawed all abortion and some forms of birth control. Congressional hearings on the bill were chaired by John East, North Carolina's co-Senator with Jesse Helms. Senator East's hearing prohibited anyone who supported abortion rights from testifying.

Myself and five other women: Stephanie Roth, Libby Smith, Tacie Dejanikus, Maureen Angelos, and Karen Zimmerman signed up independently at a forum sponsored by CARASA (Committee for Abortion Rights and Against Sterilization Abuse) to do an action inside the hearing. We had never met as a group before; some of us did not know each other; and some had never been politically active before. We planned our action in the car on the way down to D.C.

We called ourselves The Women's Liberation Zap Action Brigade. We made hand drawn signs and folded them up in newspapers, waited on line, and got into the hearings. This was in the days of live TV and before CNN. We sat in the audience and listened to speaker after speaker endorse The Human Life Statute. Then, when a male doctor testified that "a fetus is an astronaut in a uterine space ship," we couldn't take it any more. We stood up on our chairs and yelled, "Stop these hearings!"

We were so nervous that Tacie's sign was upside down. We said, "A woman's life is a human life," and we were arrested by the D.C. police and charged with "disruption of Congress" and later brought to trial. We were the lead story on all three network news shows and raised, I believe, $25,000 in contributions from people who had seen our action on television. This was before ACT UP and direct action was a contested tactic, one that eventually led to some of us being ejected from CARASA. More to the point of this story, the police officer who arrested me was named Billy Joe Picket. And in my trial he testified, under oath, that I had stood up on my chair and said, "Ladies should be able to choose."

This is fascinating. I said, "A woman's life is a human life," and he heard, "Ladies should be able to choose." I assume that the idea that a woman's life is a human life was so inconceivable to him that he couldn't even hear those words in that order.

Don't be like Billy Joe Picket. Please don't change the words or meanings of this book in order to be able to contain them. Please do not claim that I said or believe any of the following things:

> I am not saying that all families are terrible to their gay members.
>
> I am not saying that straight people don't have family problems.
>
> I am not saying that all gay people replicate and extend the arm of familial, social, and cultural oppression to each other.
>
> I am not saying that no novel by an openly lesbian writer with primary lesbian content has ever been published by a mainstream press.
>
> I am not saying that no therapist ever helped anyone.
>
> I am not saying that every gay parent is appropriate for custody.

Basically, I am not making any unnuanced arguments that are without exception. So, please don't feel compelled to be

like Billy Joe Picket and pretend that I have in order to dis-
qualify my work.

Here is what I am saying:

Familial homophobia is unjustified.
Societal homophobia is unjustified.
Cultural homophobia is unjustified.

All of these are manifested in a kind of shunning or exclusion
in which the gay person is diminished and humiliated.

People are scapegoated because they have no power. The
perpetrator realizes, or subconsciously understands, that
scapegoating this person will have no negative consequence
because no one cares enough about what happens to them to
make the perpetrator accountable. That gay people, themselves, can extend this active abandonment to each other
through a re-victimization that follows the same patterns.
Therapy does not currently provide a solution to this. The
visibility of gay people has not significantly changed this
situation.

Change lies with third party interventions to create a
critical mass of consequences for the perpetrators of shunning, scapegoating, and bullying. Third parties have the responsibility to tell families, governments, cultural arbiters,
and ex-lovers that they can no longer scapegoat the gay person and must instead practice negotiation and due process.

For example, the way AIDS activists who did not have AIDS disrupted government agencies who were shunning and neglecting people who did have AIDS, until they were forced to negotiate.

I do want to say that despite the current ideology that victims cause their own oppression, some people are really victimized. And some people are really perpetrators.

- A victim is a person who is being punished but hasn't done anything wrong, and no one will intervene to end the punishment.
- A perpetrator is someone whose behavior creates negative consequences for a person who does not deserve to be treated that way by them.
- Injustice is when the consequences of actions on another are not how that person deserves to be treated.
- Success is opportunity at one's level of merit. More than that is privilege, less is deprivation.

Some perpetrators know what they are doing, and others lack enough awareness to see what they are doing. Some defend their right to violate others; some use the awareness to change their behavior. But victims do not seek violators. They simply are more vulnerable to violation because it is known that no one cares how they are treated. It is the power of suggestion. As we learned in the anti-rape movement, the rape victim is never at fault for having been raped. The rape is always the fault of the rapist. People of color never justify racism. Simply by being born, human beings have an essential right to have their experiences acknowledged accurately; they have the right to due process in all realms; they have the right to negotiation, to express the consequences of other people's actions on them. They have the right to be included in their own family/society. They have the essential right for others to show cause before inflicting punishment.

Human beings have the profound duty to intervene when someone else is being victimized, especially if that person asks them to. Just because a perpetrator says you should not intervene doesn't mean that you have to do what they say.

Telling victims that their abuser is wrong does not help anything. You have to tell the abuser herself. A moral person creates consequences for other people's cruelty so that scapegoating can no longer continue.

When I was in fourth grade, we had a poster on the wall with a quotation from Abraham Lincoln:

"To sin by silence when they should protest makes cowards of men."

Yes that's true, but it does more than corrupt those who themselves reward perpetrators with silence. It keeps the abuse going and it abandons the victims. Silence is the greatest reward a perpetrator can receive, whether the perpetrator is a family, a government, a publishing company, or an individual. Saying nothing while your friend's family or lover or society or cultural institution shuns and scapegoats her is to participate in the process. Yes, it would be better for you, spiritually, to tell the truth to the perpetrator. But, more importantly, her chance for a decent life depends on it.